In Praise of Blandness

Proceeding from Chinese Thought and Aesthetics

François Jullien

Translated by Paula M. Varsano

ZONE BOOKS · NEW YORK

2008

© 2004 URZONE INC.
1226 Prospect Avenue
Brooklyn, NY 11218

Originally published as *Eloge de la fadeur* © 1991 François
Jullien. Published by arrangement with Editions
Philippe Picquier and Sea of Stories International Rights
Consulting Agency.

Printed in the United States of America.

Distributed by The MIT Press,
Cambridge, Massachusetts, and London, England

Library of Congress Cataloging-in-Publication Data

Jullien, François.
    [Eloge de la fadeur. English]
    In praise of blandness: proceeding from Chinese
thought and aesthetics/ by François Jullien; translated by
Paula Varsano.
    p. cm.
    Includes bibliographical references (p.) and index.
    ISBN 978-1-890951-42-9
    1. Aesthetics, Chinese. 2. Philosophy, Chinese. I. Title.
BH221.C6J85   2003
181'11 — dc21   20033057183

Contents

Translator's Preface

In 1991, François Jullien asked his readers to rethink their assumption that blandness — the absence of clearly identifiable flavor, character, or color — is an undesirable quality. This is the deceptively simple challenge he poses in *In Praise of Blandness: Proceeding from Chinese Thought and Aesthetics*, a work categorized by its publishers as an "essay" and, as such, representative of what Tzvetan Todorov has declared to be the sole literary genre in France to have thus far escaped a "generalized decline." According to Todorov, the best essayists of our time (and he counts Jullien among them) are those who "are content to analyze the world around them from a critical perspective, in the best sense of the word."[1] And for Jullien, perspective is everything — not just in the present, relatively early work, whose very title demands a radical and sustained shift in point of view, but in his philosophical project as a whole.

Blandness, like his earlier works *La Valeur allusive* (Allusive value, 1985) and *Procès ou creation* (Process or creation, 1989) and most of the works that have appeared since, singles out and explores a specific "strategy of meaning" operating within traditional Chinese literary and philosophical culture, in hopes of setting in motion a continuous reexamination and recalibration of European cultural compasses and of the practice of philosophy in the West. Recognized professionally as a sinologist, Jullien has frequently and publicly asserted that he came to this field not out of a passion for things Chinese but out of a desire to gain a clearer perspective on the roots of his own tradition as found in Greek philosophy. He describes his lifelong foray into Chinese philosophy as "a never-ending detour" and recently told an interviewer that his motives in studying China were and are exclusively "anti-exotic and theoretical," spurred by the recognition that, simply put, the only way to clearly see the self is from the outside. Why did he find in China the preferred "outside" venue from which to look back in? He offers three reasons: its philosophy is expressed in a language not shaped by the Indo-European syntax and etymology that so powerfully molded Western philosophy; China was not historically influenced by Western civilization until late in its history; and, finally, Chinese thought is preserved in a rich storehouse of texts that are still extant — and, he adds, "texts are what I had learned to work on."[2]

A cursory survey of his work over the last twenty years bears out his avowed commitment to the text; his studies and essays are invariably based in philologically grounded readings. But, contrary to the apparent simplicity of his explanation, this practice is not merely a matter of habit; it grows out of a conviction that the local, repeated linguistic expression is among the most reliable points of access into a vast philosophical system. The most obvious example of this approach may be his 1992 book, *The Propensity of Things*, in which he exhaustively explores the semantic range of the Chinese word *shi*, traditionally translated as "tendency" or "potential," and finds there the expression of an "illuminating logic" that underlies much of Chinese thought and that, most telling, is able to reach beyond the confines of its own cultural specificity and "illuminate something that is usually difficult to

8

capture in discourse: namely, the kind of potential that originates not in human initiative but instead results from the very disposition of things."[3]

For those familiar with Chinese philosophy, *shi* may not at first have seemed an obvious subject for extensive examination. So much more remains to be said, and is being said, about more persistent (not to say fetishized) terms like *ren*, *li*, and even *dao*. The book successfully puts any such doubts to rest, arguing persuasively not only for the significance of this concept in the development of Chinese thought but for its usefulness as an analytic tool. Jullien's choice of *shi* — and blandness, for that matter — as a subject of extended rumination is as much guided by its absence from Western philosophical discourse as by its presence in the Chinese. What he is looking for are "possibilities of thought" that have not yet been contemplated by his own philosophical forebears. While Jullien has acquired and continues to creatively apply the tools typically found exclusively in the workshop of the professional sinologist, his goal is considerably larger: the recasting of the types of questions that philosophy writ large can pose.

This is not to minimize his contribution to the study of traditional Chinese civilization. Whatever his ultimate goal, Jullien's excavation of such far-reaching strands of thought and strategies of meaning as found in the notions of indirect signification (*La Valeur allusive*; *Detour and Access*, 1995), efficacy (*Traité de l'efficacité* [On efficacy], 1996), and immanence (*Figures de l'immanence* [Figures of immanence], 1993) constitute interesting sinological questions in their own right — questions he poses in full engagement with the work of other sinologists in France and abroad. It will be the reader's call as to whether these lines of interrogation derive directly from the author's outsider status vis-à-vis Chinese culture, as he claims. And it is not hard to find equally overt comparative studies by American and Chinese-American sinologists;

Stephen Owen, Pauline Yu, and Andrew Plaks are among those who come readily to mind. But at a time when the American academy is increasingly preoccupied with the question of who has the right to make what kind of assertions about whose tradition — when the assertion of the right of self-representation occasionally threatens the ability of all members of the scholarly community to openly inquire into differences as well as similarities — the argument, whether explicitly or implicitly made, that those who were not born into Chinese culture also have something worthwhile to contribute (not despite but because of their outsider's perspective) cannot but enrich the range of questions asked and answers proposed.

This approach, especially Jullien's openly proclaimed "use" of China, however self-consciously adopted and passionately justified, worries readers who fear a return to the bad old days of Orientalist exoticism — bad old days that we are right to consider not yet fully behind us. The essence of the charge, as described by one of Jullien's most vocal critics, is that by looking exclusively for difference, he lays the epistemological groundwork for producing a skewed image of a China that exists only as a foil for our own civilization.[4] Without a doubt, it is a charge worth raising, especially since, in laying the groundwork for his project, he has not hesitated to draw inspiration from European thinkers not exactly known for their clear-eyed, dispassionate view of Chinese civilization: Gottfried Wilhelm Leibniz, Blaise Pascal, and, in modern times, Michel Foucault and Roland Barthes. Although Barthes comes up for criticism in the opening sections of *In Praise of Blandness,* Jullien asserts that his "own philosophical dream is, in sum, nothing other than a continuation of Barthes's, by different means."[5] He points to a passage in Barthes that he considers one of his "guiding texts" (*texte phare*), a text in which Barthes imagines the

Aristotelian tradition to which he is heir as a network of constraints from which he yearns to break free:

> The dream: to know a foreign (strange) language without, however, understanding it: to perceive in it difference without that difference's ever being recuperated by the superficial sociability of language, communication, or vulgarity; to know, positively refracted through a new language, the impossibilities of our own; to learn the schema of the inconceivable; to undo the "real" under the effect of other categorizations, other syntaxes; to discover unsuspected subject positions in speech and to alter its topology; in a word, to descend into the untranslatable and there experience the shock, never to be absorbed until all the West within us shakes and trembles and the rights of our father tongue — the one that comes to us from our fathers and makes us, in turn, fathers and proprietors of a culture that history, precisely, turns into "nature" — waver.[6]

This apparent hymn to willed ignorance and cultural self-absorption hardly seems an appropriate point of departure for someone bent on opening up new lines of philosophical inquiry. Yet starting point it is, in that it indicates a new direction only to be, itself, left behind. The present essay, and Jullien's work as a whole, do not shun understanding, but they do try to avoid appropriating for one's own language what has been understood in another. Always the desired effect is to make it and keep it strange, and then to extend that strangeness back to the language and culture that had previously seemed so familiar, so natural, so perfect a tool of analysis. Then, from that newly transformed perspective, one is presumably drawn to look once again at the consequently transformed "foreign" language and culture and thus embark on an unending spiral of inquiry (or, as Jullien has more recently described it, cycle of "respiration" — breathing). Jullien's project is

11

not to resurrect a new-and-improved monolithic Other that we can call upon at will to glorify or, alternately, demonize the Self, but to discover, through reciprocal, continual *dévisagement*, or scrutiny, the "creases" that have formed in our — and in all — thought systems.

True, it is certainly possible to extract from his work a list of cultural oppositions that might just as easily be used to point up the "impossibilities" inherent in Chinese philosophical discourse,[7] but to do so and look no further would be to stop midstream and end up at just the place that Jullien would like to avoid. Rather than a list of comparisons, says Jullien, what we need to create is a more open "montage." Precisely because Chinese thought lies historically outside the framework developed by Western thought, direct comparison is not possible; but a sustained dialogue between potentially like and unlike elements should be. "One must not confuse 'elsewhere' with 'difference': China is *elsewhere*, beyond the European sphere — it is not more different from Europe than it is similar to it; [China] is, from the outset, *in*different [in regards to Europe], their perspectives remaining at a distance from each other."[8]

This distinction between elsewhere and different, while theoretically convincing, is not so easy to perceive, let alone put in practice. Keeping in the spirit of gaining perspective through the exploration of complements, we might turn briefly to Jun'ichiro Tanizaki's 1933 essay, *In Praise of Shadows,* which bears a title similar (and arguably deals with a phenomenon related) to Jullien's *In Praise of Blandness.*[9] An elegy for an inexorably passing world, Tanizaki's writing raises the mystery of the darkly burnished and nearly unseen — of the spare and the all-but-absent — over Western modernity (a pleonasm, from his perspective) as an innately superior aesthetic, wholly more suitable to Japanese physiology and temperament. Point for point, laid out in an appropriately idiosyncratic and unpredictable order, readers find (only slightly ironic) paeans to the disappearing Japanese outhouse and laments for the encroachment of crass chrome and porcelain, the replacement of candlelight by electricity, of shoji by glass panes...of frail, thin women by plumper, sleeker models. The heartfelt meditative flow of the writing, the undeniable elegance and beauty of the images invoked, and their predictable resonance with modern readers' equally predictable nostalgia, all make it easy to accept the unabashedly simple shadow-versus-light, wood-versus-chrome, us-versus-them vision. And even after seeing through the seductive veil, we remind ourselves that Tanizaki was writing as an artist, for effect, and not as a scholar-philosopher on a quest for knowledge; we would naturally expect greater circumspection and subtlety in the latter.

But Jullien, though not an "artist," also refrains from designating his work with a title that would encourage readers to expect academic circumspection. To write "in praise of" something hints at an ironic or provocative stance — or, alternatively, an elegiac one. In the first instance, one is put in mind of a long line of "homages to" and "praises of" conventionally disparaged things: from Erasmus's praise of folly to Oscar Wilde's doubly ironic defense of lying, and, much more recently, Jorge Luis Borges's praise of darkness. Provocative in a different way are titles that make a point of lauding those indisputably "good" things that most people recognize as not receiving (or no longer receiving) their due. Library shelves are full of poetry anthologies, historical surveys, political essays, biographical essays, and literary criticism that include this expression in their distinctly polemical and non-ironic titles: *In Praise of Black Women* (translation of *Hommage à la femme noire*), *Eloge de la créolité*, *In Praise of Education*, *In Praise of English*, *In Praise of Enlightenment*, *In Praise of Hands*, to offer a sample. In these latter cases, it is common to find that the author is pointing, either regretfully or joyfully, to what she perceives as a neglected or disappearing value, drawing attention (in that way thought to be representative of postmodern thinking) to the fractures within her own tradition.

Clearly, the rhetorical tenor of the praise depends on the perceived status of its object. And few contemporary readers raised and educated in the West would identify blandness as an easy value to embrace. Its negative association with the attribute of taste is particularly resonant for the French reader, bringing to mind Anthelme Brillat-Savarin's *Physiology of Taste* (and its own slightly sardonic title), that monumental homage to the pleasures of the table and, most important, to those wise and admirable men and women who applied themselves to refining and indulging their appreciation of such pleasures. Jullien's choice of blandness as an object of extended praise would, then, seem to fall squarely in the ironic tradition of an Erasmus or a Borges — or a Tanizaki: that is, one in which the lines of opposition are clearly drawn and only one side is truly acceptable.

But Jullien's stance is more complicated than either the ironic or the elegiac; he is pointedly directing his praise across cultures, and his title's playing on our readerly reflexes is perfectly consistent with his larger aims. Potential readers unacquainted with Chinese culture (that is, his explicitly targeted readership), intrigued by the link of the vaguely repellent "blandness" with another, unfamiliar tradition of "thought and aesthetics," will then suspend their judgment that the "praise" is necessarily ironic. Instead, they will rightly consider it an invitation to reexamine a basic assumption, a conventional, native value, in the more global and relativizing framework of cross-cultural comparison. At the very least, they will find themselves entertaining, if only for the moment, a hybrid view of this as-yet-undefined notion of the bland: a dual perspective that permits movement between the ironic and the elegiac, just as it moves (in a more explicit and continual trajectory) between two cultural perspectives. Also, in this same spirit of dynamism, instead of a unifying, focused explanation of an as-yet-ambiguous, if not confounding, expression, the title promises an itinerary: an open-ended, qualifiedly personal meditation that leads to the realization — put forward within the first few pages — that "[t]he longer we pursue it, the more we come to realize that such a motif, initially so disconcerting, is fundamentally natural; it has always been there, present within us." And as one would therefore expect, the book places that process of meditation at center stage, even as it offers significant insights into the proposed subject of Chinese aesthetics.

The open-ended dynamism put into play by the title also aptly fits — indeed, performs — the subject at hand: blandness (*dan* in Chinese), the aesthetic embodiment of both the Confucian Mean and the Daoist Way, is the very image of flux within stability, stability within flux. Far from lacking anything, the blandness discovered here grows naturally out of a philosophical and aesthetic striving for what Jullien describes as "plenitude." Refusing the fixedness and consequent limitations of either conceptual or visual definitions, it retains in their place an infinite potentiality — and potency — most consonant with the moral and spiritual visions expressed in the earliest Chinese philosophical texts.

In Praise of Blandness loosely traces the gradual passage of the elusive value of blandness from its first appearances in early ritual and philosophical writings — specifically, in texts associated with the Daoist and Confucian traditions — to its gradual integration in discussions of literary and visual aesthetics in the late-medieval period and beyond. Readers interested in acquiring a historical sense of this evolving notion through time will not be disappointed; but, as the author cautions us in his opening pages, he is not interested in presenting an academic book on cultural history. Out of respect for the nature of this particular subject, he has produced here the least academic of all his full-length works (even as he does adhere, somewhat idiosyncratically, to some academic conventions). Perhaps because of this, the book has the potential to spark the interest of a wide readership.

The primary intended audience of the original, French version is the philosophically minded general reader raised with some knowledge of Western (especially French) culture and minimal exposure to the Chinese. Those who have read the occasional Chinese poem in translation or visited exhibits of Chinese painting and calligraphy, and have been puzzled and intrigued by them both, are well served here. *In Praise of Blandness* offers a productive way of articulating and thinking about some of their questions: a way of thinking that, as Jullien hopes, is likely to inspire respect for the existence of unexplored approaches to the world. This fluid encounter with blandnesses Chinese (and, to a lesser extent, Western) will not confirm these readers in their exotic, unformed ideas of Chinese culture; it is more likely to spark the desire to see more, to test this new reading — applying it both to those Chinese objects that had seemed so simple yet beyond their grasp and to the more familiar furnishings of their everyday world. It may or may not spark the recognition in themselves of traces of a value that they would never have thought of naming in just this way. But subsequent visits back to that anthology of Chinese poetry or museum exhibit — and to Western poems and exhibits — will certainly leave them with something akin to the "lingering flavor" of blandness itself: an infinite opening onto the breadth of human expression and taste.

Readers coming to this essay with some knowledge of traditional China (whose interest in questions of philosophy and aesthetics has already led them beyond the field of the familiar) will be rewarded by their willingness to hear some of their acquired knowledge recast for the explicit, but not exclusive, benefit of the lay reader. They might already be acquainted with the ideal of the "plain and bland" (*pingdan*) as an appealing, understandable response of Song dynasty literati to, among other things, their own historical latecomer status, arriving as they did on the tail of their lofty predecessors of the golden age of the Tang. But here they will see this understanding recast in a broader and more significant framework, as Jullien demonstrates the philosophical underpinnings of this label so commonly and easily associated with Song dynasty taste. And like those readers who are less knowledgeable about Chinese culture and history, they may find that their appreciation of the bland has gone beyond anything that can be so easily labeled.

Beyond the question of the benefit of this essay to specific readerships, we might ask whether it achieves its goals. Does this essay — in its blend of open-ended, not quite impressionistic ruminations and textual analysis — contribute to Jullien's unending project of constructing a living, breathing montage of Chinese and Western ways of thinking rather than a binary list of contrastive attributes? Do his straightforward adoption of the outsider stance, his unsystematic and rhetorical references to Barthes, G. W. F. Hegel, Paul Verlaine, and Vladimir Jankélévitch, and his unabashed selection of difference encourage or discourage the ongoing readjustment of cultural and philosophical perspective that Jullien purports to promote? Does the subjective eye of the essayist enhance or detract from our free exploration of the blandness he unfurls before us?

My own feeling, one that guided both my decision to translate this book and some of the specific choices I made in the translation, is that the answers to these questions depend on the orientation of the individual reader. Those inclined to categorically refuse contrastive comparisons can expect to come away from this essay armed with vehement and easily substantiated objections that not everything in Chinese culture fits into the category of blandness: for these readers, proof positive that the category of thought presented here is merely a construction of the author's self-serving obsession with difference. But readers will reap greater benefits if they can, for example, perceive the fruitful paradox in Jullien's eminently unambiguous — "unbland" — treatment of his subject and in his forceful authorial, and culturally specific, presence. Perhaps, as foreshadowed in his title, the initial shock of the Tanizaki-like polemical praise of blandness will effectively jolt readers into a truly open exploration — "*proceeding from* Chinese thought and aesthetics." Perhaps the reader is best able to disentangle his own path of discovery from that of the author when the latter is most clearly demarcated. The personal voice is one that expects an answer, one that incites an inner dialogue that, if properly conducted, effectively mirrors the kind of dialogue that lends both depth and honesty to openly transcultural explorations. For all readers even marginally interested in the still-unanswered question of how to approach, ethically and openly, a culture not their own, Jullien's essay (even if it strikes some as too self-accepting) provides a provocative model for continued discussion and elaboration.

Finally, there is the question of the translation itself. What is the best English rendering of the word *dan* — which Jullien rendered as *fadeur*? Initially, I would have liked to find an English word that signifies a lack of flavor and that at the same time benefits from the positive connotations supplied by a culture that honors the presence of absence. But then there would probably be no need for this essay. The French *fadeur*, for all its identification with the absence of color and taste, seemed to suggest at least the possibility of something positive. Somehow, it still retains (at least to the ears of this nonnative speaker of the language, an impression I confirmed with native speakers of French) a certain poetic elegance — and perhaps not merely because of the term's association with Verlaine. But English incarnations of the idea all seemed impossibly repellent; not even previous occurrences of "blandness" and "insipidity" in scholarly works on Song dynasty poetics and painting allayed my concern that, whatever term I chose, nonspecialist readers would interpret the title as meaning "in praise of the inherently uninteresting" –and react accordingly.[10]

English is hardly lacking in approximate equivalences for *dan*. But words with negative prefixes or suffixes ("flavorless," "colorless," "indistinct") indelibly imprint the idea with the image of something missing and so irresistibly and misleadingly draw attention to that missing something. "Dilutedness" appeared at first to be a particularly felicitous equivalent of the Chinese character; *dan*'s etymological and textual associations with water lend this choice a certain authority. But aside from the word's clunkiness, so antithetical to the impression that *dan* should convey, the inscribed past participle inaccurately suggests that this quality resulted from the transformation of some other original (and thus more natural) state. A similar problem arose when considering the word "fadedness." The neutral expression "plainness" seemed a viable option, as did "faintness," "discreetness," and "paleness"; but I ultimately decided that they inadequately convey the original term's primary allusion to flavor and, by extension, to the faculty of taste. Only a word with gustatory associations would do, both for its immediate and visceral comprehensibility and for its adherence to the earliest metaphoric uses presented by Jullien in this essay. For those purposes, I could find nothing that surpasses "blandness."

Another, more profound challenge derives from the style of this essay. Jullien's writing accommodates his avowed determination

not to betray the value of blandness by fixing it in a repeatable, aca-
demically acceptable formula; he would like to avoid offering the
assurance of philosophical discourse. He makes this point explicitly in his Prologue but gives us a detailed justification of this concern only later, in Chapter Nine, when his readers have had some
time to come to terms with the elusive bland. Here, in a discussion
of the work of the fourth-century poet Ruan Ji, he reveals his own
preoccupations:

> How, we might ask, can one speak of blandness? Is it possible to
> explore it in essay form? Would it not be more in keeping with the
> very logic of this subject to simply decline to develop it verbally (for
> fear of fixing it in an overly emphatic, definitive discourse) and aban-
> don any justifying arguments (in order to avoid slipping back into
> false contradictions)? This would, after all, avoid the risk of distort-
> ing something that, by definition, does not obtain as a discrete, iden-
> tifiable object of discourse (and we recall in this regard that the word
> "bland," or *dan*, also signifies inner detachment). Discourse, being
> what it is, only serves to heighten particularity, to demarcate with
> ever greater precision — and I want to speak of the neutral, the indif-
> ferent, the transitory.

Indications of Jullien's desire to slip the bonds of formal, orga-
nized discourse are apparent at many levels of this essay, from his
smooth integration of fragmented, expressionistic sentences to
his broad strokes as he moves through history and across the diverse genres of philosophy, music, poetry, painting, and calligraphy. The personal voice of the erudite essayist who wants to
persuade and provoke the imagined resistant reader, more than
the systematic presentation of irrefutable proof and logic, is what
determines both the tone and the flow of this piece. In his desire
to reach readers unfamiliar with Chinese culture, Jullien tried to

spare them the burden of footnotes and a host of unfamiliar (and, for many, unpronounceable) proper names; and when he felt obliged to provide such names, he avoided distracting readers with biographical details.

In translating this essay, I have tried to capture the personal tone of the original. Likewise, in working with Jullien's translations of classical Chinese texts, I have tried to respect his choices of style and level of language. However, anticipating that much of the American readership would appreciate easy access to concise contextual information about the Chinese philosophers and artists he discusses, I have provided that information in an appendix. Having done so, I have also, on occasion, taken the liberty of inserting the names of these historical figures in the essay (in brackets) where appropriate; however, as the reader will discover, the thrust of Jullien's argument in no way relies on recognition of any but the most frequently mentioned. In addition, I have provided references for all quoted Chinese texts, along with some clarifications and annotations (again in brackets), for the convenience of scholars in the field of Chinese studies. Finally, for readers of Chinese, I have followed Jullien's example in providing a character glossary of all cited Chinese terms and expressions (which appear in the essay in Pinyin romanization).

Prologue

The quality of blandness: no sooner do you identify it than it begins to appear at every turn. Blandness, by definition, pays little heed to the borders our various disciplines like to draw among themselves. As the embodiment of neutrality, the bland lies at the point of origin of all things possible and so links them.

Like a bland flavor, the merit of which lies in not being fixed within the confines of a particular definition (and in thus being able to metamorphose without end), the motif of the bland recurs ever anew in Chinese culture, never succumbing to containment or delineation. It is a beneficiary of each of the three schools of thought (Confucianism, Daoism, and Buddhism); and it evokes an ideal common to the arts of music, painting, and poetry.

In order to convey this quality of blandness, whose sole characteristic is to elude characterization — to remain discreet and unobtrusive — I have had to attempt to avoid engaging in the usual weighing and measuring. This is why I have refrained from developing this intuition into an object of scholarly inquiry and put aside (literally, in endnotes) indications of sources and references. But such omissions do not constitute an act of simplification (if only because there is nothing here to simplify; rather, the simplicity of things eludes language). We live in an age of standardized

cultures, of "channel-surfing" among civilizations and "digests" —
even as meaning is lost the moment that its unique historical itinerary ceases to be taken into account.

For these reasons, I hope to bring the reader as close to concrete examples and original texts as possible so that he might
experience for himself a bland sound, a bland sense, or a bland
painting. I hope he might benefit, too, from as much detachment
as possible so as to better interpret this experience; to this end,
I attempt to situate these different cultures in relation to one
another and to gradually develop some bases for comparison.

I began reflecting on this question ten years ago, but limited it
to the narrow confines of a subchapter of my doctoral thesis.[1]
Since then, it has appeared to me to be both much more central
and more inclusive, extending across many fields besides my own.
As the Chinese have always said, if "all men are able to discrimi-
nate among differing flavors," the blandness of the "Mean" (or
the "Dao") is "what is most difficult to appreciate." But it is precisely this that lends itself to infinite appreciation.

And so I began to rewrite.

Blandness: that phase when different flavors no longer stand in
opposition to each other but, rather, *abide within* plenitude. It
provides access to the undifferentiated foundation of all things
and so is valuable to us; its neutrality manifests the potential
inherent in the Center. At this stage, the real is no longer blocked
in partial and too obvious manifestations; the concrete becomes
discrete, open to transformation.

The blandness of things evokes in us an inner detachment. But
this quality is also a virtue, especially in our relations with others,
because it guarantees authenticity. It must also lie at the root of our
personality, for it alone allows us to possess all aptitudes simultaneously and to summon the appropriate one in any given situation.

On this common ground of the bland, all currents of Chinese thought — Confucianism, Daoism, Buddhism — converge in harmonious accord. None of these systems conceives of it as an abstraction (for the purposes of establishing a theory) or, at the opposite extreme, as ineffable (in the service of some mystical calling). But it is precisely the bland that the arts of China reveal to us through their uncluttered spareness and allusive depths.

By taking us to the limits of the perceptible, that place where perceptions assimilate and nullify each other, the bland brings us to experience a world beyond. But this movement does not open up onto another, metaphysical world, cut off from the senses. It simply unfurls and expands this world (the only one): drained of its opacity, returned to its original, virtual state, and opened up — forever — to joy.

CHAPTER ONE

A Change of Sign

First, one accepts the paradox: that to honor the bland — to value the flavorless rather than the flavorful — runs counter to our most spontaneous judgment (and elicits a certain pleasure in thus contradicting common sense). But in Chinese culture, the bland is recognized as a positive quality — in a class, in fact, with the "Center" (*zhong*) and the "Root" (*ben*). The motif of blandness emerges early, in the thought of ancient times, whether in composing a portrait of the Sage or in evoking the Way. Ever since, it has permeated and enriched the Chinese aesthetic tradition — not just because the arts in China have benefited from the fruits of this intuition in the course of their development, but also because the arts can facilitate our perceptual apprehension of this basic blandness. Indeed, it is their mandate to reveal it; through music, poetry, and painting, the bland is transformed into experience.

When the seemingly paradoxical becomes self-evident, when the value of the bland has changed signs, we begin to feel more comfortable and familiar with Chinese culture. When we begin to apprehend the stirring — beyond our ideological reflexes and cultural conditioning — of the *possibility* of a positive notion of the bland, we have entered China: not into its flashiest or most sophisticated realms, but into what is most simple and essential.

In this sense, we can appreciate the usefulness of this motif. Its distinctiveness does not emerge from a theoretical construct, parallel to the less-than-complex representations of "Chinese thought" we invent for ourselves (to be understood in relation to our opposite page: "Western thought"). Rather, we recognize it immediately, within ourselves. It requires nothing more than to apprehend, at the core of our judgment, this alternative path. And, indeed, just how "other" is it? The longer we pursue it, the more we come to realize that such a motif, initially so disconcerting, is fundamentally natural; it has always been there, present within us.

When Roland Barthes returned from his 1975 trip to China, he brought back nothing more than a few pages (reissued by Christian Bourgois under the provocative title *Alors la Chine?* [What about China?].[1] We recall how, in a similar quest during the same period, his encounter with Japan had so stimulated his passion for signs [resulting in the publication of *Empire of Signs*[2]]. In telling contrast, these few pages about China convey nothing so much as his reserve, his silence. He did not evince any interest in discovering other signs, or another hermeneutic; rather, he seems to have found pleasure in noting a lack of signs, in observing the *"suspension"* (his emphasis) of our sensual avidity:

> And so we leave behind the turbulence of symbols and approach a country that is immense, ancient, and yet very new, where meaning is so discreet as to become a rarity. From this moment on, a new territory is revealed: that of delicacy, or, better yet (I venture using this word, at the risk of having to take it up again later), of blandness.[3]

There is something significant in how he ventures using the word "blandness" here. He makes it clear that he preferred this word to other, more common words, even as he withdraws it in advance, pronouncing it temporary. Barthes is tempted by an inversion of the sign (a positive blandness) but does not dare — or cannot? — follow it through to its logical end. He will correct himself later with "a more accurate phrase": "China is peaceful."[4] (And at the end of the Cultural Revolution no less — is this really possible?) Most likely, Barthes knew nothing of the motif of the bland as it has evolved within the Chinese tradition. But he did notice something that he develops provocatively, within the limit of those pages, as his guiding theme. China is not "colorful"; it is "flat," "pale." There, words harbor something "silent," and "amiability" remains "distant." In short, for this lover of rhetoric, China is "Prose."[5]

Rereading those pages today, we are surprised. Side by side with statements that are simply untrue (which, in fact, the author strives to avoid saying, doubtless because he senses their ideological conformity: his "leftist intellectual" prejudice in favor of the Cultural Revolution), we find something else that, because it is *felt*, is quite accurate. This secondary discourse attempts to cover over the primary as much as possible but cannot (must not!) mask it completely. Hence those disastrous linguistic slippages, such as: the increasing political rigidity of Pilin-pikong "rings" in our ears "like a joyful bell."[6] Clearly, there is something we desire to understand and that we must explain, and we must not surrender it to the easy pleasure of terminological web weaving just at the moment we begin to sense its presence.

In direct contrast to Barthes's approach, let me cite Hegel. In his *Lectures on the History of Philosophy*, he introduces Confucius — "the most renowned of philosophers" ("among the Chinese") — as a sort of subaltern Cicero. According to Hegel, Confucius's interviews with his disciples can be essentially summed up as a collection of moral doctrines or "insipid" prescriptions: "Their morality is good and honest, and nothing more; we must not expect to find therein any deep philosophical inquiry" — not to mention "speculation"! "For us, there is nothing to be obtained from his teachings."

And further:

> Cicero's *De officiis* may well be more valuable and of greater interest to us than all the books of Confucius combined, for these latter are very thin and watered-down, like books of moral sermons.[7]

His conclusion: it would have been better for the Sage's reputation had "his works...not been translated."

Reading the *Analects* of Confucius, we can easily see what might have appeared so "insipid" (in the pejorative sense of the word, of course). One finds there neither theoretical definitions nor logically developed arguments; there is no systematic development of a branch of knowledge, only a succession of brief anecdotes, lapidary responses, and human-interest stories:

> The governor of She asked Zilu about Confucius, but Zilu found nothing to say. The Master said to Zilu: "Why did you not respond: 'He is a man who, in his passion for study, forgets to eat; and in his joy upon acquiring knowledge, forgets his worries. He does not sense the approach of old age!'?"[8]

The glosses provided by the most respected Chinese commentator (Zhu Xi, to whom we owe the most penetrating synthesis of Chinese thought) guide us in our reading of passages such as this. Does Zilu's silence suggest that he found the question inappropriate, or that he felt uneasy in attempting to explain "in words" what constitutes the Master's virtue? In his answer, Confucius summarizes his life as made up of two moments: that devoted to research, so fervent that he forgets all other concerns, including eating; and that spent in the experience of "joy" (by which we understand the joy at having arrived at his goal, at having found the object of his quest), so perfect that he forgets all "worries." We note that the object of his quest and, subsequently, of his happiness is never specified (this object is not only a matter of knowledge — whether of absolute knowledge or of something that can be defined and represented as distinct from one's own itinerary). What matters is that the alternation of these two moments (or, more exactly, these two movements), striving and inner contentment, infuses his life with rhythm, filling it entirely. Forgetting to eat (not the ascetic refusal to feed oneself), forgetting our cares (even while remaining involved in, preoccupied with, the world): such is the logic of the enthusiasm and self-transcendence in which existence is swept up. And in striving to raise itself up, existence eventually succeeds in making one forget its natural limit, one's approaching old age (which might also, after a short while, matter little). Is the Master smiling at himself in amusement? He does not present himself as possessing the keys to wisdom or knowledge and makes little of the results obtained, not out of modesty, but because what matters is the tension between the two movements, its renewal and duration (more than a result that, by its very nature, must be temporary). In short, what matters is that uninterrupted desire to go beyond, a desire that finds within itself its own end (its "happiness") and keeps life young and evolving.

We must "savor" this suggestion "in its profundity" (*shen wei zhi*), advises the commentator, for, beneath the simplicity of its expression, we apprehend an awareness of reality "that is total and reaches the extreme" (we are far now from that thin characteristic of moral sermons ridiculed by Hegel).[9] Is the World itself,

31

in its elemental capacity and "wondrous" renewal, any different from the faculty of eternal perseverance (from which all morality is derived)? Is it any different from this process that — because it is, as Zhu Xi also says, "pure" (neither deviating nor getting bogged down) — moves ever forward and "never ceases" (these being among the most ancient Chinese expressions for conveying that which constitutes the very basis of reality)? Unless one is the Sage (par excellence), one cannot fulfill in an enduring way this unique and absolute demand. At the same time, what Confucius says about himself enables us to understand the nature of "heaven" (as the Absolute of reality), not in a speculative sense or through allegorical transpositions, but simply through the spontaneous development of the trope, through the ceaseless, expansive movement of its meaning.

Zhu Xi concludes his remarks, saying, "Generally speaking, the ideas that the Master holds about himself are like this; it is wise to extend their meaning through the whole of his thought."[10] Were it not for this remark, one might wonder at finding, several paragraphs later in this book, that the Chinese revere above all others this kind of sentence:

> When the Master sang in the presence of his companions, if one of them happened to sing well, he would ask him to begin again, and he then would accompany him.[11]

A small detail (to become, as such, the object of a separate discussion), but one that allows us to apprehend, says our commentator, "the Master's open, relaxed manner" (that is, he does not disdain this type of pastime and is always ready to learn from others).[12] At the same time, our commentator tells us, we discern therein "the highest degree of inner authenticity" (intent as the Master is on judging most fairly — and in practice — his own abilities) and "perfect modesty"; the Master does not hesitate to let the talents of others shine forth. "A small point of information," then, but one that "contains all of the Master's fine qualities." "They can never be exhaustively recounted," admits the commentator. And so we conclude once again with this nonconclusion: "It is for the reader to savor it in its details."[13]

Isn't what had been judged "insipid" from a speculative standpoint (that is, the Hegelian standpoint) thus revealed as the most savory? We see here how a characterization that seemed at first blush decidedly bland (and therefore unworthy of our extended consideration) can give rise to the richest variations and the farthest-reaching applications. Now meaning can never again be conceived as closed and fixed but remains open and accessible. It is wise, then, to train oneself in this art of reading: an approach that allows for an *infusion* of meaning, a far cry from the imperious enumerations of (demonstrative) discourse and all its unrelenting classifications and distinctions. Such a mode of reading allows the full potential of meaning to gradually infuse the reader as he puts himself at the disposal of its secret urgings and embarks on an endlessly renewed journey.

The motif of the bland distances us from theory but does not, at the other extreme, commit us to mysticism. True, we have acquired the habit of allowing faith to pick up where reason leaves off. Still, if for the Chinese blandness does not lend itself to abstract constructs, neither does it form the basis for a categorical rejection of all discourse and a leap into the Ineffable.

This is because, with the bland, we remain in the realm of perceived experience, even if it situates us at the very limit of perception, where it becomes most tenuous. The bland is concrete, even if it is discreet: hence the ability to evoke it in landscape.

CHAPTER TWO

The Landscape of the Bland

In the foreground, only a few sparsely leaved slender trees clearly indicate the presence of vegetation. Arranged around this stand of trees, some flat rocks suggest the contours of a riverbank extending from point to point, while airy hills on the other shore unfold this level scene out into the distance. The limitless clarity of the sky answers the emptiness of the water, which spreads to fill the entire central portion of the scroll. Finally, a thatched roof, supported simply by four poles, presents the only sign of a possible human presence. But no one is sheltering beneath its eaves (figure 2.1).

The ink used to paint this landscape has been generously diluted. The range of colors is narrow, and pale overall. The strokes appear not so much in individually distinct traces as in marks meltingly submerged into forms. The painter has even refused to treat distant objects differently, as one usually does, by reducing the amount of detail or blurring the outlines. Near and far are fundamentally homogeneous, "reflecting each other," as it is commonly said, and becoming equals under the viewer's gaze. The gaze travels evenly from one edge of the scroll to the other; only the vertical lines of the delicate boughs tie together the two shores, keeping the various planes on the surface. No more impulsive

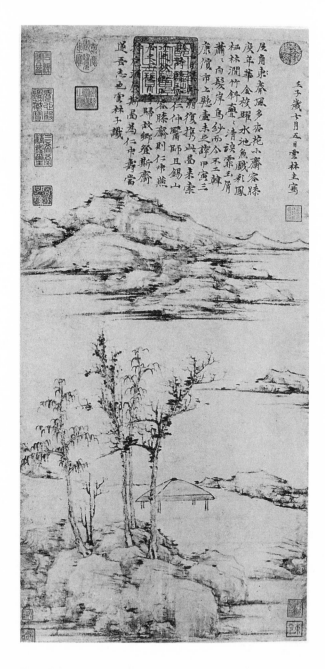

Figure 2.1. Landscape of blandness I. Landscape of Ni Zan, 1372 (National Museum of Taipei).

brushstroke than these disturbs the calm that unfolds across the different parts of the scroll; no decorative, or merely pleasing, touch relieves the platitude of the whole. Yet, drained of all opacity — unburdened of all weightiness — as such a landscape is, it does not lack its own substance and in this differs from its all-too-numerous imitations. The sketched shapes possess volume, the spottiness of the sparse dots garbs the contours in a bit of moss, and a few darker strokes delineate more clearly, here and there, the edges of things. Nothing here strives to incite or seduce; nothing aims to fix the gaze or compel the attention. Yet this landscape exists fully as a landscape. The Chinese critics traditionally characterize this in one word: *dan*, the "bland."

Trees on the riverbank, an expanse of water, some nebulous hills, a deserted shelter. The artist, Ni Zan (fourteenth century), painted virtually the same landscape throughout his life. He did this not, it seems, because of a particular attachment to these motifs but, on the contrary, to better express his inner detachment regarding all particular motifs and all possible motivations. His is the monotonous, monochromatic landscape that encompasses all landscapes — where all landscapes blend together and assimilate each other. And this is all the more evident when one considers that this painter's career evolved toward ever greater simplicity and spareness. In a work executed in his youth, dated 1339, the two banks are still close to each other, the rocks are dense and massive, and we glimpse distinct people beneath the thatched roof (see figure 2.2). In another painting dated thirty years later, the composition as a whole has not changed, but trees and mountains are treated with greater sobriety. The middle area reserved for the expanse of water has increased, and all human presence has disappeared from the pavilion (see figure 2.1).

We are familiar with Ni Zan's life and, notably, with the circumstances that impelled him to aspire to more detachment and to

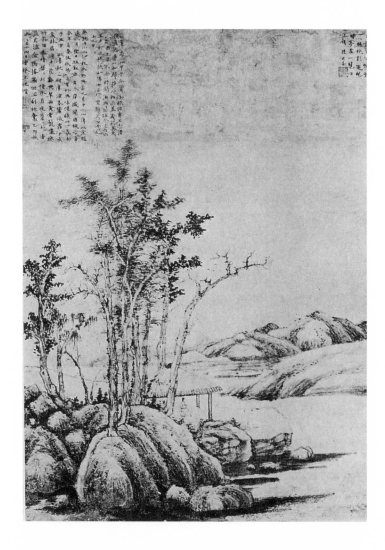

Figure 2.2.   Landscape of blandness II. Landscape of Ni Zan, 1339 (John M. Crawford Collection, New York).

favor a greater degree of blandness. Until his forties, considerable family wealth allowed him to lead the life of an aesthete. He filled his library, which he had had constructed on his estate, with rare books, antique bronzes, valuable zithers, and, of course, the paintings and calligraphic works of the greatest masters. There, living in a world where all had been purified and nothing remained of vulgarity, he received his few friends (he is even thought to have been obsessed with material cleanliness). But in fourteenth-century China, prey to the Mongol occupation, the demands of those in power became more frequent, and the taxes imposed on estates more burdensome. To avoid the increasingly weighty cares of managing a large estate, Ni Zan, it seems, resolved to change his life. He relieved himself of his possessions and spent the remaining decades of his life traveling on the waters of the lower Blue River and the Great Lake, living in a simple skiff or staying in monasteries. Thus renouncing his social position, he freed himself from the increasingly onerous burdens that, during those difficult times, were inextricable from material wealth. So, too, he was able to escape the political upheavals that accompany the fall of dynasties in China.

But he did not, for all that, isolate himself in a life of spartan solitude; he did not cut his ties with the world. Having rid himself of the burden of things, Ni Zan did not reject their presence. Open, unattached, wandering at the behest of the water's tranquil flow, traveling from friend to friend, he evolved in a world freed from all constraints, a world offered up fully to be encountered and enjoyed. The blandness of the painted landscape cannot be confined to the realm of artistic effect. Rather, it expresses wisdom, for the bland life constitutes an ideal.

CHAPTER THREE

Blandness-Detachment

Ni Zan's biographers teach us that, at the end of his life, his knowledge of Daoism deepened and he lived at that time in close contact with a meditating sect connected with Maoshan. I am well aware of the artificiality involved in summarizing a life by affixing to it the name of a school of thought, especially in China. I know, too, that there is something simplistic in expecting to open the drawers of known doctrines, one by one, and find there the justification of an intuition that both encompasses and supersedes them all. Nevertheless, it is in connection with the "Dao" — the term that comes both first and last in the thought of Daoists — that the motif of the bland begins to possess a special significance in China. Indeed, it does so in a number of decisive expressions that profited from the tendency, characteristic of this school, to play with paradoxes and to turn commonly held opinions upside down. From the beginning, the motif of the insipid took part in this widespread reversal of values that aimed at evoking the essential.

According to the Daoists of antiquity, the very foundation of reality, in its infinite fullness and renewal, reveals itself to us as "bland" and "flavorless" (*dan hu qi wu wei*):

Music and things dear and delectable
stop the passerby in his tracks.
When it passes through [that is, "comes out of"] the mouth,
the Dao is insipid and flavorless:
it cannot be perceived,
it cannot be heard,
but it is inexhaustible.[1]

All flavors disappoint even as they attract. Persuading the passer-by merely to "stop," they lure without fulfilling their promise. They represent nothing more than an immediate and momentary stimulation that, like sound sifted through an instrument, disappears the moment it is consumed. In contrast to such superficial stimuli, the bland invites us to trace it back to the "inexhaustible" source of that which constantly unfolds without ever allowing itself to be reduced to a concrete manifestation or completely apprehended by the senses: that which transcends all particular actualizations and remains rich in virtuality.

Every actualization constitutes a limitation, for it excludes all other becoming. It will never be anything more than that particular flavor, the given flavor, compartmentalized in and restricted by its insuperable particularity. In contrast, when no flavor is named, the value of savoring it is all the more intense for being impossible to categorize; and so it overflows the banks of its contingency and opens itself to transformation.

From this arise the turns of phrase that turn language against itself, ostensibly taking a stand against common sense: the Sage "savors the flavorless" (*wei wuwei*) and "busies himself" with "nonaction."[2] Wisdom consists in perceiving that opposites, far from being sequestered in their exclusive individuality, ceaselessly modify and communicate with each other. The one never transpires but in response to the other, and all reality is nothing more than this process of reciprocal engendering. Art and wisdom consist, then, in allowing oneself to be led from one extreme to the other, intervening as little as possible, in order to benefit fully from the logic — inherent in the real — constituted in this dynamic of reversal. One must not apply oneself to resolving "difficulties" at the stage when the situation has become difficult. Rather, we are shown, one anticipates the predictable arrival of this stage and pays close attention to things while they are still easy to manage. Neither should one desire to realize immediately any "great projects"; instead, always begin at the incipient stage of things, which, as such, constitutes a promise of development. In the same way, one must not seek flavor in flavor itself, since it is, in its very essence, relative, ceasing to be detectable as soon as it is identified. One must allow oneself to be brought to true flavor from that phase which is its opposite: blandness. Blandness, as it evolves, tends naturally toward flavor, which, in turn, far from remaining in barren isolation, opens itself to its own superseding, revealing itself as an infinite progression.

This blandness, as experienced in things, corresponds to man's capacity for inner detachment. That the same Chinese word — *dan* — signifies both, without distinguishing between subject and object, invites reflection. It is also, from this moment on, what gives on this opposition its great inclusiveness: flavor provokes attachment, and insipidity provokes detachment. The former overwhelms us, clouds our minds, reduces us to a state of dependence; the latter liberates us from the pressure of the external world, from the excitement of sensations, from all false and short-lived intensities. It frees us from fleeting infatuations and silences the wearying din and clamor. And with this act, our interiority, inseparable from the apprehension of the world's blandness, recovers its quietude and serenity and evolves all the more freely for it, for when consciousness no longer permits itself to be ensnared by the diversity of flavors but perceives the essential non-differentiation at the base of all these differences, the world can again open up to its initiatives. Fixations and blockages disappear. Desire's overdeterminations and the encumbrance of things evaporate as well, and all of one's faculties work together spontaneously and freely.

This has nothing to do with the morality prescribed by loners living in retreat from the world. Indeed, the lesson reveals itself as being most valuable in the realm of politics and is applicable to business management as well. In one Daoist parable, Root-of-Heaven, hoping to learn how to govern men, goes to consult Man-Without-a-Name in the country of *yin* and *yang*. The nameless one insults his visitor, offended at being disturbed just as he was preparing to "go forth with the Creative Principle," to fly off beyond the world's boundaries to the land where "nothing exists anymore." Then, because Root-of-Heaven repeats his request for knowledge, he responds:

> Let your heart move freely in blandness-detachment [*dan*] and unite your breath with non-differentiation [*mo*]. If you cleave to the spontaneous movement of things without permitting yourself to entertain individual preferences, the whole world will be at peace.[3]

The phase of "non-differentiation" is that from which all things originate and to which all things return. And so the virtue of blandness lies exactly in making our spirit coincide with this most basic of all phases. As long as no one flavor attracts us more than any other, and one is not favored more than another, we maintain an equal balance among all the virtual forces at work (for example, our sense of *qi*) and let the logic inherent in existence play itself out naturally, on its own. Preference alone is the source of trouble, and only favor is flawed. They cloud the transparency of the natural process and scramble the just designation of things. In contrast, the leader to whom all things in the world appear of equal blandness can, because of his interior detachment, renounce intervention, preserve his regulating immanence, and thus cause peace to govern the nation.

Like emptiness, tranquillity, indifference, insentience, or non-action," then, blandness-detachment characterizes the basis of reality and serves as the platform on which all existence rests. Therefore, it is vital that we not take an absence of flavor or allure as a sign of deficiency, not to mention as an indication of a negative theology (of the Absolute); the blandness that leads to detachment is simply the path of free, unimpeded growth, the path of what happens spontaneously. This blandness-detachment places us at the point furthest from Revelation. Recall Christ's injunction to his disciples: "Ye are the salt of the earth: but if the salt have lost his savour, wherewith shall it be salted? It is thenceforth good for nothing, but to be cast out, and to be trodden under foot of men."[4]

In this tradition, salt is a sacred condiment and at the same time the mark of difference — even of categorical opposition. One used to speak of the "salt of the covenant" or of an "covenant of salt" to suggest its incorruptible and venerable character; one would talk about "eating the salt of the palace" to express a man's belonging to his Lord. But here our taste of the real is not brightened by any calling, not seasoned by any message. Reality projects no meaning beyond itself, and nothing else lends it variety or attraction. Blandness characterizes the real in a way that is complete, positive, and natural.

CHAPTER FOUR

The Sense of Neutrality

The analytic constructs that necessarily emerge in the course of writing intellectual histories often compel us categorically to oppose Daoists and Confucians, as though one side could be defined in terms of spiritual aspirations and the other in terms of society's demands. But I believe that the Chinese motif of blandness leads us to transcend this type of rigid distinction, and it is precisely in this capacity that it is so promising. Not that we no longer need to consider the differences in language (or the articulation of what, precisely, is at stake) between the two schools. But through the motif of the bland, we are inspired to look beyond such categories to perceive the manifest nature of things, never in question, on which these two schools are based. We are compelled to go beyond the usual debates to examine the common basis that underlies them both and permits them to engage in a dialogue at all. After all, the valorization of the bland belongs not only to the Daoist celebration of an original nature; we encounter it in the Confucian portrait of the Sage as well.

In effect, both schools pursue the same line of inquiry, asking what constitutes "the foundation of Heaven and Earth" — the "root" of all that exists, as it is commonly expressed. Confucians, after all, are no more anxious than Daoists to oppose being and appearance, or to separate the rational from the empirical. No metaphysical preoccupations here (at least not until the arrival of Buddhism), for this philosophy does not engage in ontology. Indeed, it seems to me that we must proceed from this very point if we are to gain an understanding of ancient Chinese (as opposed to Greek) thought.

This approach to the real does not encourage inquiry into what truly *is* (the "in-itself" or the "Idea"), and thus it is never called upon to change. Rather, the Chinese perspective opens directly onto the coherence inherent in change itself and so bestows on becoming the logic of its own transpiring. The Chinese are interested in accounting for the *potential* (*de*) common to all reality and for all its stages of existence, from the subtlest to the most apparent — without which the world would not be continuously renewing itself and without which life would cease its course. What, then, is the source of the efficacy of change? This is the question posed at the start. And what is the origin of the regularity on which this harmonious functioning depends?

In the eyes of Confucian literati, if nature's cycle (or "Heaven") is to endure and grow in fecundity without ever being depleted, and if the virtue of the Sage is to operate and exert its influence unceasingly on all that exists, then it is essential that neither Heaven nor the Sage deviates from its or his respective path or veers toward one side or another. All such partiality, in both senses of the word, bespeaks a corresponding lack in or retreat from the inherent capacity of the real to communicate through and throughout itself, to incite and to respond (that is, to react constantly in the sense of *gantong*), and, by virtue of that ability, to maintain itself ever in process.[1] When this capacity is thus compromised, there appear a corresponding decline in vitality and all manner of barriers to the *continuum* of the real. Under these conditions, opacity and inertia — apathy and sterility — arise in things as well as in consciousness itself (indeed, these deviations constitute the only "Evil"). And as for Heaven and the Sage, their only virtue consists in their never allowing themselves to be restricted or blocked. It is a virtue that, almost by definition, depends on the ability to maintain at all times the position of centrality (zhong), which alone permits a reaction to the totality of a given situation and the avoidance of both excess and insufficiency and encourages the full development of the capacity to "bring about" (cheng).

The Confucian ideal, then, has nothing to do with the "mediocrity" of the middle of the road — aurea mediocritas, or faint-hearted prudence — with which it is so often confused. Nor can it be reduced to an Aristotelian "mean" (mesotès, Nicomachean Ethics 2.5), which is uniquely moral in nature and pertains only to the realm of emotions and actions. Rather, it is based on the perception of the fundamental neutrality of all nature — that of the world as well as that of man. Insofar as man originates in the supreme font of reality ("Heaven"), he naturally finds himself in this position of perfect centrality. All he need do to ensure that "Heaven and Earth are in their proper places" and that "all beings flourish," then, is to keep his emotions in harmonious balance.[2] There is no other basis in reality apart from this value of the neutral: not leaning in one direction more than in another, not characterized more by one quality than by another, but preserving, perfectly whole within itself, its capacity for action. From this neutrality derives, in the eyes of Confucians, all true efficacy. And to the neutral we owe, of course, the ineluctable blandness that is the mark of the Sage.

But how, we may ask, can the neutral be detectable, how can it manifest itself in a particular way? In effect, the virtue of the Mean, although immanent in all things, does go unnoticed, because it eludes the characterizations (whether of excess or insufficiency) imposed solely by our inclinations.[3] Or rather, it goes unnoticed precisely because this immanence (that of the Dao) is universal. It can only be identical with itself and so never betrays the existence of distinctions or distances. As it is commonly said, "rare" are those who can "gain awareness of it": it presents no telltale identifying marks, boasts no remarkable "flavor," and blends in with the normal state of things. A *banal* virtue. It is at one and the same time most valuable and most common; it is that through which all is realized, remaining all the while absolutely invisible. If from the standpoint of human behavior it constitutes the goal most difficult to maintain, it is nonetheless also the most ordinary of ideals, one that is within everyone's reach — within the reach of the "everyday couple." Confucius himself protested against the all-too-easy cult of the extraordinary:

> Attempting to live differently from others [or, according to another interpretation: attempting to penetrate the mysteries of the most obscure], along with trying to accomplish miracles so that future generations have a reason to speak of one — now, here are things that I myself will assiduously avoid![4]

We read in ancient treatises of the military arts that just as good military strategy contains nothing that can be praised, the true Sage proffers nothing that can be duly reported; he exercises his virtue close at hand, within his family and in the day-to-day, such that the benefit of his actions never attracts attention, never offers a sign or mark of its existence. Relating as one intimate to another, he brings about, almost imperceptibly, the evolution of an antagonistic situation, so that the gradually attained victory never calls for admiration and is never referred to as a great accomplishment. True efficacy is always discreet; conversely, the ostentatious is illusory. Sage and strategist alike reject spectacular and superficial acts in favor of an influence that operates profoundly and over time.

On the side of the instantaneous and evident: flavor. On the other side, the side of things that remain diffuse and obscure (but all the more effectual): the bland.

And so the virtue of the Sage cannot be perceived externally. That is why the Sage's portrait begins with an opposition between its inner vibrancy and the dullness of its manifestation:

> According to *The Book of Odes*: "Over her brocade vest, she adds a simple robe of a single color." This is because she does not want to reveal such an ornate article of clothing.
>
> In the same way, the Dao (that is, the Way) of the gentleman, because he prefers to remain in the shadows, grows more brilliant with each passing day; whereas the Dao of the small man, because he prefers to shine, grows ever dimmer.
>
> The Dao of the gentleman is bland but never wearing; it is simple yet ornate; it is flat but not lacking in harmony.
>
> He who knows the nearness of that which seems remote, he who recognizes whence arrives the wind [as influence], he who is conscious of the manifest becoming of the most subtle — he can accede to virtue.[5]

The less evident a quality, the greater its capacity to grow. Plenitude is all the greater for its refusal to show itself. And let us take care not to misunderstand; this is not remotely a question of humility. Rather, this restraint is the very condition for non-exhaustion. Simplicity and plainness are the just measure of authenticity, which is situated at the opposite pole in relation to the flavorful — whose intensity and seductiveness are doomed to wear themselves out. The "blandness" of the Sage, however, is "never wearing" (*junzi zhi dao dan er bu yan*).

Several phrases in the passage above confirm, it seems to me, just such an understanding of the bland. That the "remote" begins near at hand or, as it is said elsewhere, that "in order to go far, one must set out from nearby" (or "leave from the foot of the mountain in order to reach the summit") reminds us that even the most extreme result — the most far-reaching and remote — begins to realize itself close by, in simplicity.[6] The virtue of the Sage, as we have seen, is perfectly plain and ordinary, and accession to true flavor, that is, blandness, must occur gradually (we note that in politics in particular, the benefits of virtue spread from intimate to intimate, from associate to associate, and from the family to the world at large). The phrase "whence arrives the wind" suggests that the Sage's influence is all the more vast and potent for not being apparent as something separate and distinct. The quality of the flavorful lies not in its particularity or in its substantiveness but only in its diffuse capacity for penetration and its power to move through us. The phrase "manifest becoming of the most subtle," finally, tells us that true flavor is not a pure state but something continuously deployed, growing ever more appreciable and pervasive. As a result, the strongest presence is conveyed in the greatest reserve.

Rather than isolating the various aspects of the real, the stages of becoming, and setting them against one another, the Sage understands that the existence of extremes expresses something else, something more fundamental: that everything exists only in process, in its passing from one state to another. From this we understand the importance of qualifying existence in terms of the bland, the only category capable of denoting this state of continuous transition. While flavor establishes opposition and separation, the bland links the various aspects of the real, opening each to the other, putting all of them in communication. The bland renders perceptible their shared character and, through this, their primordial nature. Blandness is the color of the whole, as it appears to the eyes of those who look farthest into the distance; it makes us

experience the world and existence itself beyond the narrow confines of the individual's point of view — in their true dimension. If
blandness is the flavor of sagehood — its only possible flavor — this
is not because the Sage has grown resigned or disenchanted but
because blandness is the most basic and authentic of flavors: that
of the "root" of things.

Chapter Five

Blandness in Society

"The Sage is bland but never wearing": this statement applies especially well to our relations with others. Here, too, we find ourselves before an intuition that is common in China, as expressed in the proverb "Dealings with the Gentleman are as bland as water, while dealings with the small man are as pleasing to the taste as new wine."[1] If Confucianism and Daoism vary in their applications of this comparison, it is only because of differences in style, intention, and context.

The Daoists dramatize this in a way that is deliberately polemical and loaded with irony. In the following passage, Zhuangzi presents a Confucius who, disappointed in life, has gone to seek an old sage (Daoist, of course) to whom he can recount his woes:

Twice I was expelled from the state of Lu. In Song, they cut down the tree under which I was sitting. I am no longer allowed to set foot in the state of Wei, and I was reduced to extremes in Shang and Zhou. I was trapped between the countries of Chen and Cai. And then, on top of these misfortunes, my parents and my relatives have less and less to do with me, and my disciples and friends are abandoning me more and more. Why has all this happened to me?[2]

To Confucius's tearful laments the old Daoist responds with an anecdote. A man from Jia, fleeing from his country in ruins, chose to rid himself of a jade disk worth a thousand pounds of gold so that he could carry his newborn child on his back. This, he reasoned, makes sense because what binds the infant to the man is a natural link. "All who join together merely for reasons of common interest reject one another when oppression, despair, ill fortune, grief, or disaster strikes."[3] But confronted with the same bad luck, those bound by a natural link only grow closer. In effect (and here the argument becomes especially persuasive), those not bound together because of common interest will never have any reason to break those bonds. That is why it is said:

> Dealings with the Gentleman are as bland as water, while dealings with the small man are as pleasing to the taste as new wine. The blandness of the Gentleman solidifies his friendships; but the vulgar man, because of his sweetness, destroys them.[4]

The same critique of the flavorful, then, arises here, but from the Daoist standpoint, which opposes all that does not accord with the spontaneous, guileless movement of our nature. Blandness is the measure of this true naïveté: free from intention and thus never short of the mark. In contrast, social conventions, and all other false values imposed by civilization, stir within us interests and desires that, being completely artificial, are the most volatile. If vulgar relations seem at first "pleasant to the taste," it is because they depend on such stimulation; and so their flavor is obviously artificial. The author concludes his anecdote with the conversion of Confucius, putting an end to clownish hypocrisy and false wisdom. "Confucius returned home unhurried and serene. He renounced his studies and gave up his books. His disciples stopped performing the rituals of reverence, but their love for him grew."

This satiric depiction notwithstanding, upholders of Confucian ritual, too, put forward the ideal of blandness in human relations, doing so in the name of personal sincerity and loyalty to others (in the sense of *xin*). The Gentleman does not intend to mislead, never speaks of what he can do, and views the little courtesies of the day-to-day as at the furthest remove from the true exigencies of propriety:

> When the Gentleman finds himself in the company of a man engaged in observing the funerary rites of one of his parents, if he is not able to help him with a gift, he does not ask about the cost. When he is in the company of a man who has an invalid at home, if he is not able to give him something to help feed that person, he does not ask him what he would like. Finally, when someone comes to visit, if he cannot offer him his hospitality, he does not ask where the visitor plans to spend the night.
>
> Relations with the Gentleman are like water, those of the small man like new wine. The Gentleman is bland, but that is why he is able to bring things about; the small man is pleasant [to the taste], but that is why he ends up only destroying things.[5]

Now, a change in style and setting: here, we are far from the free-and-easy manner of the Daoists, far from their facetious — even provocative — tone. But if the Confucian presentation is not quite as dazzling, its significance is no less profound. Indeed, just this quality conveys the profundity of the ordinary: blandness. The Gentleman does not pretend to care about others if he is not able to help them or match his expressions of concern with action. Whereas the Gentleman subordinates his words to his actions, the vulgar person seeks only to make a good impression. The sweetness of this flavor tempts us, draws us in; but it is false, lacking in righteousness and rigor. Only on the basis of reserve, modesty, and discretion can one "bring about" reliable human relations that do not disappoint. One does not bring about that which one cannot sustain; nor is it to lapse into self-righteous moralizing to believe that only effective realization counts and that the facts themselves have the last word. "To bring about," *cheng*: Confucians situate it in the context of human relations (rather than in relation to the virtue of "Heaven" and as a capacity inherent in nature), but their preoccupation is the same as the Daoists'. The blandness of others, which is for us a guarantee of authenticity, brings us back to the universal value of the neutral.

CHAPTER SIX

Of Character: The Bland and the Plain

We can also praise the blandness of the Sage from a psychological, rather than a moral, perspective. Blandness should be our dominant character trait, since it alone allows an individual to possess all aptitudes equally and to bring the appropriate faculty into play when needed. From this perspective, the nature one might speak of is no longer human nature, always growing, understood in its universality and proceeding from its transcendental basis of reality (as in the well-known phrase "That which is ordained by Heaven is nature").[1] Rather, it is the "natural" (*caixing*) belonging to each one of us and discernible through the attentive observation of behavior, of a person's attitude or face. This point of view is also more empirical, appealing to subjective evaluation and judgment, in the sense of *pin*. After the founding of the empire in 221 B.C.E. (that is, the Han dynasty, which put an end to the period we refer to as "antiquity" in China) and the establishment of an extensive bureaucracy, we notice an increasing interest in evaluating the respective merits of individuals as the practice develops of grading the officials' aptitudes (after which appears the grading, in an analogous system of "superior," "average," and "inferior," of the relative talents of calligraphers, painters, and poets). On this scale of abilities, "blandness" ranks the highest:

In general, in human character, centeredness [as in the ability to remain in the center — *zhong*] and harmony are most valued. And in order for a character to be centered and harmonious, it must be plain, bland, and flavorless. This type of character is thus able to coordinate the five aptitudes and adapt smoothly to all situations.[2]

Only a person's "blandness" and "flavorlessness" (*pingdan wuwei*) make it possible to simultaneously encompass contradictory qualities. As the commentator of the *Renwuzhi*, cited above, explains, only blandness allows the coexistence of the "five flavors," sour, bitter, sweet, sharp, salty: "When the flavor is bitter, it cannot at the same time be sweet; when the flavor is sour, it cannot at the same time be sharp."[3] Thus only blandness ensures the perfect polyvalence of character that allows an individual to meet all aspects of a situation at once and to cleave to it smoothly in its evolution. In another note from our commentator, "when a man's character is plain and bland and does not exhibit any particular proclivities, then he is master of all his abilities and uses them most effectively: he adapts himself to all changes and never encounters an obstacle." The error would be for one quality to dominate; this, once again, is "partiality" (*pian*) — inclination in a particular direction, the source of trouble.

In my view, we can never be too conscious of the originality and uniqueness of this Chinese psychology of blandness, this refusal to allow any single trait to affirm itself to the detriment of another: in short, this esteem for completeness by determinacy. No single aptitude, whatever it might be, should monopolize the personality as a whole, and it is less a matter of energetically pushing a situation in a given direction than of exploiting it by molding oneself to it. The ideal is not a no-holds-barred offensive in which all efforts are directed toward a single goal, but an individual's openness, which moves in harmony with the fluctuations of the world and makes it possible to partner them freely. Instead of a situation where a particular exertion causes all inner resources to contract and gush forth before our eyes, these inner resources remain in a state of repose, maintaining their equilibrium and blending into blandness.

This lesson of the bland, the insipid, also applies to political life. Traditionally, Chinese literati, by virtue of their vocation, expect to assume an official position; the only alternatives are either to engage in or to retreat from official life. And since nothing in the personality of the Sage is overdeveloped, since he never feels himself to be predisposed more toward one particular stance than another — and is therefore open to all eventualities — he *can* enter into public life or retreat from it with as much flexibility as possible, as the moment requires.[4] One could well declare this to be opportunism, and, in effect, it is opportunistic. But it is essential not to misread its underlying ethic: any virtue to which we attach ourselves or that we consider more important than others, however valuable, constitutes an inner fixation that will block the renewal of our personality, calcify our subjective dispositions, and sterilize our nature. In contrast, the blandness of the Sage makes it possible for him to embrace all virtues without being subjugated by any one in particular and to remain ready, throughout the inevitable fluctuations in political life, to face calmly and serenely the most pressing issues of his day. Like Heaven, he may well seem to change often, but he never deviates from his course.

And so we are hardly surprised when the preceding passage concludes as follows:

> This is why, when observing a man and judging his character, one must first examine his ability to be plain and bland, and only then inquire into his intelligence.[5]

The term we translate broadly here as "intelligence" (*congming*) actually suggests the dual ability to hear and to see. Here, implied in language itself, is the idea that — in another instance of blandness/plainness — any given quality can only be effective insofar as it forms part of an inner equilibrium. Thus intelligence as understanding-perspicacity is the result of the joining of hearing and vision, of a correspondence between inner and outer, of a harmony between *yin* and *yang*. At the core of human personality, the effect of this compensating balance should extend beyond interactions among the "five abilities" (which are analogous to the "five flavors" and correspond to the "five elements") to the dualistic structure of each one of these abilities (for example, righteousness and flexibility, softness and hardness). And beware: emphasizing one aspect over another will not benefit the one emphasized but will actually act to its disadvantage. As it grows in size and importance, that ability will limit its own field of action. Implemented in moderation, however, it can operate with greater precision and subtlety (in the sense of *jing*) and without impediment.

This psychological praise of blandness is further supported by a semiotic justification. All inner qualities possess their unique signs through which they recognizably manifest themselves in the world: through comportment, attitude, countenance, and even the more general aspect of the face, voice, or the expression conveyed in a look. Thus in one who possesses all these qualities in equal amounts, no external sign can express itself to the detriment of any other, no particularity can reveal itself; in short, his personality will present nothing that might be perceived by others as striking or remarkable. This has been eloquently formulated: "When the 'five abilities' are fully present, the personality is enveloped in blandness."[6] The commentator further specifies that "then there is no dominating flavor." The expression of the personality is not directly "expressive" but clarified, refined, "limpid."

The perfect character is without character, its plenitude inseparable from its platitude. At the same time, the new attention brought to the "perceptible expression" (*zheng*) of an invisible reality, to the concrete expression of the "dimension of the spirit" (*shen*), as well as to its various corresponding "symbols" (*xiang*), testifies to the fact that at around the third century, a unifying vision of the real — at once cosmological, moral, and political — begins to arise in China. An appreciation of signs for themselves also emerges as sensitivity to the value of blandness begins to move in the direction of an aesthetic sensibility.

This appreciation of blandness in character is not merely the result of psychological theorizing. We find it inscribed in the contemporaneous biographies of well-known figures whose air of detachment and serenity permits us to infer an inner richness. It shows, too, in Chinese statuary of Buddhist inspiration, then just beginning to flourish, which we can still admire in sanctuaries carved in stone, such as those in Datong (figure 6.1). "The facial type is flat and bland," Osvald Sirén tells us, "barely exhibiting the slightest degree of modeling." We do not recognize "all the gravity, classical reflection, urbanity" of the Gandharan style from which these sculptures draw their inspiration. Nevertheless, as Sirén also tells us, this "almost nonexistent" modeling of the facial features "suggests a certain inner harmony." These works produce an impression that is "naturally fleeting," and very dependent on the effects of lighting, "but not negligible; rather, it is revelatory enough to ensure that the spiritual order of the best sculptures of Yungang has remained strong down through the centuries. It remains fresh and pure in gray and desolate surroundings."[7]

Elusiveness of impression but also durability, limpidity, and spirituality, even in the midst of surroundings that are "gray and desolate": just so many complementary facets of the sign of blandness beginning to take their place in a work of art.

Figure 6.1. Blandness in portraiture. Standing Buddha (Datong, Cave XXIII).

CHAPTER SEVEN

"Lingering Tone" and "Lingering Taste"

Gradually, starting in the third century, critical writings appear that begin to separate the didactic, moral uses of art from its effect. We know that an aesthetic sense had already been developing for quite some time, but it did not at first assert itself independently; rather, its expression still depended on pragmatic justifications. At times, it might be in the context of developing a political idea that one would invoke, as a comparison, the delicate task of seasoning different flavors; or that one would identify water, which later became a common trope for blandness, as the "original" element, the basis for all other flavors; or that one would demonstrate awareness of the "ineffable" character of the harmonious blending of the different tastes; or that one might pronounce as ideal the subtle balance which determines that "spiciness is not sour" and "blandness is not too light."[1] At other times, it would be in the course of developing a moral idea (if one can even make a distinction between the moral and the political in such a context) that one might appeal to that fertile contradiction underlying the assertion "that which is empty can, at the same time, be full; and that which is bland is, at the same time, full of flavor" — like the man who "carries a piece of jade beneath vulgar clothes."[2] In the following passage, which reflects on two forms of education — rites and music — the argument for blandness, from the specific viewpoint of the experience of savoring, is more explicit:

> This is why musical perfection does not consist of the greatest deployment of tones and [proper] ritual offerings to the dead do not consist of the richest, most complex flavors.
>
> The strings of the zither upon which "Qingmiao" [a musical piece played in ancient times during ritual offerings to the ancestors — TRANS.] was played were of vermilion [strings that were boiled, thus producing a relatively muffled sound — TRANS.], and the body of the instrument was loosely assembled [that is, the base still had hollows in it, causing the sound to resonate longer — TRANS.]; one lone singer began, and only three others accompanied him. Nevertheless, the lingering tone was strong. In the ritual offerings to the royal ancestors, dark liquor was placed in the highest position, and on the tables raw fish was presented. The great broth was not seasoned; still, it left a lingering flavor.

According to the commentators, the vermilion cords — woven of boiled silk and so not very taut — emitted a sound that was "muted" rather than ringing. Leaving the pieces of the zither loosely assembled also served to produce a sound that was "slow." Finally, by specifying that one singer carried the melody alone and was only accompanied by three other singers, the passage depicts a musical concert at its most unadorned, for it is performed without the participation of a chorus. "Nevertheless, the lingering tone was strong." For, the most beautiful music — the music that affects us most profoundly — does not, as is mentioned at the beginning, consist of the fullest possible exploitation of all the different tones. The most intensive sound is not the most intense: by overwhelming our senses, by manifesting itself exclusively and

66

fully as a sensual phenomenon, sound delivered to its fullest extent leaves us with nothing to anticipate, nothing to look forward to. Our very being thus finds itself filled to the brim. In contrast, the least fully rendered sounds are the most promising, in that they have not been fully expressed, *externalized*, by the instrument in question, whether zither string or voice. And it is thus that they manage to sustain (as formulated in this lovely expression) a "lingering" or a "leftover" tone (*yiyin*). Such sounds are all the more able to extend and deepen themselves in the minds of their hearers for having not been definitively realized; and so they retain something more for later deployment and keep something secret and virtual within. In short, they remain heavy with promise. As noted by the commentator, music such as this stays on in the spirit and "is not forgotten."[4]

The same holds true for the experience of taste. The most solemn ritual sacrifice (such as offerings to the royal ancestors) is reduced to the greatest simplicity: the fish is not cooked, the great broth is not seasoned. Such simplicity is, in and of itself, a sign of solemnity; in addition, it is the least pronounced flavor, the least seasoned dish, that possesses the highest degree of *potential* flavor. Exactly like the leftover tone, the "lingering" or "leftover flavor" (*yiwei*) evokes a potential, inexhaustible value, ever more desirable as it continues to avert its own consumption.

Flavor or tone, expanded by virtue of its own discretion, kept open to becoming by virtue of its own reserve: what it loses in physical manifestation, it gains in spiritual presence. The text goes on to show that the practitioners of these rituals were interested less in "completely satisfying" the desires of ear or palate (that is, in quenching the yearnings of our bodily organs) than in guiding men to develop a feeling for the Way. The juxtaposition of the two types of music — one that dazzles the senses and one that awakens consciousness — is as venerable in China as the conflict of Orpheus and the Sirens and the resentments of Platonic thought are here in the West. This passage shows clearly how moral reflection, which we can still detect in the background, served to support the increasing valuation of blandness. But just as clearly, this articulation of blandness also contains an analysis of our receptive capacities and of sensual experience, which is ripe for application in the realm of aesthetic reflection. And so it will be applied, as the motif of lingering or leftover taste or tone extends beyond the realm of music to that of poetics.

CHAPTER EIGHT

Silent Music

Let us remain wary of facile comparisons. Beneath the banality of "common ground" (such as that found in the themes of morality or music) lies hidden a much more fertile and original intuition. While the ethical significance of music is a well-worn subject in many ancient societies, and is found in Greece as well as in China, the Chinese rejection of the full and complete exploitation of sound does not lead to Plato's classic opposition between corrupt music (too expressive, sentimental, or languid) and music that is favored because it is weightier, more solemn (*Republic* 3). True despite the fact that this same opposition does appear in China; the condemnation we find there of the airs of Zheng and Wei for their negative influence on morality resonates with Plato's damning judgment of the styles of Ionia and Lydia.[1] The lingering tone upheld by the Chinese tradition affirms the value of music itself, not merely its capacity to exert a positive influence (on society). The lingering tone simply increases music's already assumed power and beauty.

Nor is the preference for discretion in tonal production based on a metaphysic of musical experience as conceived, for example, by Plotinus (developed in the course of *Timaeus*) or the Church Fathers. As expressed by these latter, the significance of music lay elsewhere than in its status as an aural phenomenon, which they considered meaningful only insofar as it was allegorical. For them, it was as if there existed some inaudible, celestial melody superior to the ones we perceive physically — as if "the music of perceptible things" were created "by a music anterior to it" and sprang from it (*Enneades* 5.8.1); indeed, it was as if the music perceived by the ear carried an encoded message revealing the mystery of the Invisible. The Chinese view is unacquainted with the opposition between the perceptible and the rational conceived of as two distinct realities, of which one is a copy of the other; it is unthinkable that music might originate in another world, whether that of the Spheres or that of the angels.

Since in this view the only difference lies in the relative subtlety of music's production and effect, that which is coarse enough to be picked up by the senses lies on the same continuum as that which is too subtle to be perceived, accessible only to the spirit (*jingshen*) — that other, finer "organ." In its coarser, cruder state, reality presents itself as fragmented, limited, opaque; but when in a state of high refinement, it "communicates" throughout (*tong*), operates free from both breaches and blockages, becomes limpid. And this state forms the basis for the one preceding: it constitutes the shared "stem," rooted in the Invisible, from which the profuse "branches" open out, like so many sensitive extremities.

If, then, the leftover tone and its lingering resonance are preferable to the full exploitation and immediate consumption of sound, it is because they bring us — through *perception* — to a subtler and more fundamental grasp of reality. They recall our spirit from its state of dispersion at the still-complex and coarsest level — from the "branches" — back toward an intuition of that shared and discreet simplicity that lies at the beginning of things and remains just under the surface. The physical dimension of tone is not denigrated in favor of transcendent paradigms or music of other worlds, but it does have to yield to its own deepening into silence — by exceeding its own boundaries.

This intuition is, again, that of ancient Daoism. Let us once more take up the comparison opposing the *root* of the stem to the tips of the *branches* (*benmo*) and apply it to music. If the "bells and drums" of the orchestra and the steps of the accompanying dance constitute the "branches" of the musical phenomenon in its entirety, it is because this state — the final one — of the playing of instruments and of aural and visual manifestations is only the culmination, stylized and tangible, of a capacity for harmony, the efficacy of which is to be sought further up the continuum, by tracing back the sounds themselves.[2] While melodic virtuality remains whole and limitless, once we come to the "thusness" of concrete actualization, any music, once performed, presents only a particular, fixed exteriorization, analogous to the use of punishment and reward in any educational process (which it only sanctions), or ritual weeping and mourning clothes in relation to the infinitude of grief. Those who remain attached to such spectacular and stylized manifestations lose sight of the profound sense of phenomena. The five notes of the scale can but drive men to a state of deafness, just as the "five colors will blind him" or the "five flavors will desensitize his palate."[3] Here we find some common ground with Daoism: just as he spiritualizes his vision, the Sage knows how to attune his ears to silence, and it is in the state of silence that he perceives harmony.[4]

Early Chinese thought pushed the opposition between the physical phenomenon of an emitted "sound" (*sheng*) and its capacity for harmony, or "tone" (*yin*), even further, in that it treats these two elements as a pair, like other oppositions: before-behind, high-low, great-small.[5] It is in light of this type of contrast that the following aphorism (later to become a proverb) yields its meaning: "The great harmonic — sound at its most subtle," an all but paradoxical aphorism, which, in cutting short all musical effusiveness and so all harmonic loss, enriched the meaning of music.[6]

> That which cannot be heard through listening is what is meant by "sound at its most subtle." "The great harmonic" refers to sound that cannot be heard. As soon as a sound is produced, a schism is introduced; and once there is a schism, one note exists while another exists not, and one loses command of the whole. That is why when sound is produced, it is not "the great harmonic."[7]

In the realm of vision as well, "the greatest representation" is without particular "form" (as a unique actualization); rather, it encompasses within itself all possible concretizations. The same holds true for the musical notes of the scale, for colors, and for flavors. One flavor can be more marked, but only at the expense of another; and at the moment when one musical note is sounded, it excludes all other notes. Here we recognize the adage "Omnis determinatio est negatio [Every delimitation is a negation]." Conversely, the "formless" and the "toneless" possess the ability to "communicate with all things" and to "reach all destinations."[8] True harmony can only exist in a state prior to all differentiation, because it begins by leading us step-by-step down the ladder of wisdom, as is explained in the following passage, also excerpted from the Daoist classics:

> There are among the ancients those possessed of perfect knowledge. They understood that there have never been individual beings: this knowledge is perfect and definitive, to which nothing can be added.
>
> One step beneath them, we find those who believed that individual beings do exist, but they have never possessed individual attributes. Yet another step down are those who believed that there are individual attributes assigned to individual beings, but there is no

opposition between the positive and the negative. It is with the appearance of the opposition between positive and negative that the Way is lost; and with that loss, the emergence of preference.[9]

Here, we begin to see the logical connection between two opposing but complementary sides: "emergence" (*cheng*) and "loss" (*kui*). As soon as the primordial oneness is sundered, "emergence" leads, by that very act, to destruction. We are presented with the example of Zhaowen the musician:

Emergence and, also, loss —
This is Zhaowen playing his zither.
Nothing emerging and nothing lost —
This is Zhaowen not playing his zither.[10]

As the commentator explains, no matter how talented the musician (or, for that matter, how many musicians are in the orchestra), from the moment he begins or they begin playing, some notes are lost as others are brought into existence, whereas "if it is not manifest, the sound remains integral and complete."[11] In declining to play — that is, in refusing to participate in the play of individual beings, of separate entities, of "for" and "against" — Zhaowen maintains his position in the supreme state of musicality and of wisdom.

We find a corresponding homage to musical *restraint* at the end of a dialogue between Confucius and his disciples. Now, one avoids dividing up — and thus creating an internal opposition within — the harmonic whole; now the spare, discreetly emitted notes return to silence. According to a passage in the *Analects*, Confucius one day asked his disciples, seated beside him, to speak freely about what they would do if their qualities were finally recognized and they could fully exercise all their talents. To put them at ease, he invites them to forget for a moment — and this is quite significant coming from a Master in China — that he is their elder. One disciple immediately answers with confidence that if placed in charge of a modest principality, even in the most insignificant state, he would get it back on its feet in three years' time. Another, a bit more modest, contents himself with guaranteeing within three years the prosperity of all its inhabitants, while leaving the care of their moral education to those wiser than he. A third, even more prudent, would be happy to serve as a mere acolyte during diplomatic meetings in the ancestral temple. Dian, the last of the disciples, responds by plucking a final note on the zither that he has been playing very quietly in the background all along, allowing its sound to fade out as the vibration gradually ceases. (In another interpretation, his hand, slowing down on the chords, picks out a few final notes — sparser and more tentative than those preceding — and the sound emitted by the zither laid on the ground gradually fades away.) Dian's answer, when he at last emerges from his quiet reserve, is completely different:

> Near the end of spring, dressed in our springtime clothing, I and five or six companions and six or seven young boys would swim in the Yi River, take pleasure in the wind on the Terrace of the Rain Dances, and then return home together, singing.[12]

And the Master concludes this passage with a deep sigh: "Dian, I am with you!"

As confirmed by this ending, which serves as a commentary on the dialogue as a whole, the first three answers express all the usual political preoccupations, albeit in order of decreasing ostentation and increasing indirectness. Notwithstanding each disciple's shrewd attenuation of the grand plans of the one who preceded, they all speak of their ambition to play an active role — and all wait in vain for the Master's approval. Dian's answer, however, does not build on the examples of those preceding but rejects the pattern outright, setting off in another direction entirely — situating his desire in another dimension. Yet this change of tone was contained in and foreshadowed by his initial response, ever so discreet, of the gradual extinction of a single note: in the uncomplicated return of sound to silence. The insertion of this pause, this sigh, transforms the preceding perspectives and gives voice to something else. More effectively than any articulated argument or theoretical illustration, this slowly dissipating note breaks with the previously expressed preoccupations but without aggressively insisting, as words might have done, on how petty such urgently felt wishes and desires may be. It suffices to simply disengage us from the trap of individual roles and responsibilities in order to bring us to another level of existence: not one projected into that "realm beyond" of personal ambitions, but one discovered, revealed, in the immediate realm of the harmony of the world, as perfectly in unison with men as with nature, with water as with wind; the true "vacation," and that of which Confucius himself would dream.

To refrain from even beginning to play or to allow the last notes to deepen into the inaudible: music is caught between these two aspirations, which, in devaluing its concrete reality (as being false and ephemeral), call it to an existence that is ideal in that it is complete and all-encompassing. Somewhere between its reluctance to emerge and its desire to be reabsorbed into the whole, the played tune comes about only to make it possible to experience the tacit and perfect harmony from which it emerges and into which it returns. It is the *internal* sense of musicality that matters (as opposed to its material, and thus external, production). I would like to offer, as additional evidence, a Song dynasty poem citing both Dian's and Zhaowen's attitudes, juxtaposed in a parallel couplet. In it, they are joined — despite their respective

Daoist or Confucian resonance — in their shared awareness of an ineffable harmony:

> The flowers in the vase emerge — red,
> Incense smoke rises in pearl-gray curls.
> Neither a question nor an answer,
> The *ruyi* laid obliquely on the ground.
> Dian allowed the sound of his zither to fade away,
> Zhao refrained from playing his zither:
> In all this there is a melody —
> That can be sung, and can be danced.[13]

Several clear signs help us read this scene: from the incense smoke (the dialectic of question and answer brought to the final stage of reversal and elimination of speech itself) to the *ruyi* — the "as-you-like-it" — a wand used for back scratching, left carelessly on the ground. We understand that the poem suggests Chan (or Zen, as it is called in Japanese) meditation. A much later critic praised this poem as "perfectly coherent with the situation," well known in Buddhist scriptures, in which "Sakyamuni contents himself with plucking a flower and his disciple smiles at him in response."[14] Everything in this eight-line poem conspires to surpass limits and subvert distinctions (including such divergences in opinion or in tradition as defined by Confucianism, Daoism, and Buddhism) and to eliminate all instances of exclusive individuation. The flowers appear as a single blur of red above the vase; the smoke dissipates in curls. All fragmenting of plenitude is avoided, and a "music of silence" — virtual, infinite, and thus all the more present (one to which we can even dance!) — is its fruit.

Another, equally famous motif found in the Chinese tradition tells of this same rejection of the actualizing rupture from which individual sounds are born. It confirms us once again in our

attachment to the evocative power of a music that is never manifest but is continuously suppressed. Here is Tao Yuanming, a poet
who, more than any other, is recognized in China as the poet of
the "natural." His name alone has come to signify existence freed
from all demands, having condemned them as just so much ostentation; and his verses take simplicity to the heights of ecstasy.
According to his biography in the *History of the Song*:

> Tao Yuanming knew nothing of music, but he had at home a simple,
> unadorned zither without any strings. Whenever he experienced, in
> drinking wine, a feeling of plenitude, he touched the zither in order
> to express the aspiration of his heart.[15]

His zither was left rough, unadorned, and, above all, without
strings. The poet did not have to "trouble himself" to produce
individually each note "from above the strings."[16] The body of the
instrument contains, within itself and at the same time, all possible sounds (the very image, of course, of the Dao). The media-
tion of strings and the effort of performance have been rendered
useless — have even become obstructions. The inevitable progression of a played melody along its only possible dimension, the lin-
ear, would also destroy the fundamental oneness of the experienced
harmony. At the same time that it is being actualized, as we have
already seen, each tone isolates itself and deprives itself of the others. One should not, then, attempt to distinguish among its different aspects or constrain one's emotions to their successive and
selective expression in time. But nor are we speaking of illusion,
of a purely fictive copying: there is the gesture of caressing the
zither, a gesture that is tentative yet very real, brought to life by
the universal and unified movement of the fingering of an instrument. As such, it carries the potential of all of music's musicality
and alludes to the entire harmonic capacity of all possible sounds.

CHAPTER NINE

The Blandness of Sound

Such, then, is the bland sound: an attenuated sound that retreats from the ear and is allowed to simply die out over the longest possible time. We hear it still, but just barely; and as it diminishes, it makes all the more audible that soundless beyond into which it is about to extinguish itself. We are listening, then, to its extinction, to its return to the great undifferentiated Matrix. This is the sound that, in its very fading, gradually opens the way from the audible to the inaudible and causes us to experience the continuous movement from one to the other. And as it gradually sheds its aural materiality, it leads us to the threshold of silence, a silence we experience as plenitude, at the very root of all harmony.

As we have seen, perfect harmony exists only in that moment before actualization — or, otherwise, just afterward, as it submerges itself into undifferentiation: either before or after the moment when particularities assert themselves, when specific traits delineate one another and establish their relative contrasts. That is, at that stage when the flux of existence is still unified and its tensions still latent or in the process of being reabsorbed rather than intensified. Such is the profound serenity of the Dao, in contrast with artificial ruptures and all emphatic epiphenomenality. And in the following passage, blandness and silence are the same thing:

The great Process of nature is simple and easy; likewise, the most beautiful music is uncomplicated. The virtue of the Dao is plain and bland [*dan*]; it possesses neither sound nor flavor. As the music is uncomplicated, so *yin* and *yang* communicate spontaneously; where there is an absence of flavor, all beings are spontaneously happy.[1]

These lines are from an essay in which the political-moral interpretation of music, as inherited from ancient times, still dominates. And so it does not identify the ideal of "neither sound nor flavor" as such. Also note that the quality of blandness is here applied more specifically to the Dao than to music.

But faced with the author's reticence in characterizing the ideal of blandness, we might inquire further. How, we might ask, can one speak of blandness? Is it possible to explore it in essay form? Would it not be more in keeping with the very logic of this subject to simply decline to develop it verbally (for fear of fixing it in an overly emphatic, definitive discourse) and abandon any justifying arguments (in order to avoid slipping back into false contradictions)? This would, after all, avoid the risk of distorting something that, by definition, does not obtain as a discrete, identifiable object of discourse (and we recall in this regard, that the word "bland," or *dan*, also signifies inner detachment). Discourse, being what it is, only serves to heighten particularity, to demarcate with ever greater precision — and I want to speak of the neutral, the indifferent, the transitory. We are speaking here not of an absolute ineffability (that is, in the metaphysical or theological sense: that which, by definition, transcends all language and remains incommensurable with it) but one that is *relative*: the ineffability that lies at the root of all language but that all language is destined to lose as soon as it begins to assert itself. And so the less said (that is, the more one refrains from saying), the more complete the expression of blandness. In language's erasure of itself, it acquires the ability to evoke the bland.

This is why traditional Chinese writers and artists prefer to gesture allusively toward this motif. They content themselves with simply pointing in the direction of meaning's aspired end, an end constituted, precisely, by the death of meaning. This is why musical blandness is a privileged theme in poetry, especially fitting for the end of a poem: the poetic word fades along with the sound it emits. Through evocation of this theme, the poets of the Tang dynasty later paid homage to the leftover sound that, once emitted by the zither string, spreads through the universe: the bland sound of the final chord, detaching us from performed music and disposing us toward a meditative state.

Fading sound blends with nature and opens space. In the following lines, the great Tang poet Li Bo writes thus of the beauty who sings and dances in her filmy robes of gauze:

A light breeze carries the songs into emptiness:
The melody entwines itself with the passing clouds and flies off.[2]

The spontaneous entwining of the melody with the clouds recalls a famous story from one of the Daoist classics. In olden days, a young woman on her way to Qi, having run out of provisions, sang in an inn to earn some money. After she left, "the lingering tones entwined themselves around the pillars of the house for three days running; so people nearby thought that she hadn't yet left."[3] Another of Li Bo's poems invokes the same theme but removes all traces of fleeting sensuality, emphasizing instead the theme's ambient feeling of infinitude:

The lingering tones cross the river and depart:
At the sky's edge — how can they be found again?[4]

The poem closes with a question. The other shore is just on the horizon; just as the evocation of leftover sound is inextricable from the greatest possible expansion of the landscape, the final question opens onto the immeasurable and gives access to the invisible. We notice something similar in this famous poem, also by Li Bo:

> The monk from Shu holds his zither in his arms,
> In the west, under the peak of Emei Mountain.
> For me a single strum:
> Like hearing all the pines singing deep in the valley...
> The traveler's heart is rinsed in the running waters,
> Lingering tones enter the frosted bell:
> Unheeded, on azure mountains, evening falls;
> Autumn clouds: how many layers in the dark?[5]

Maurice Blanchot, citing Martin Heidegger, compares poems emerging from the noisy world of "nonpoetic language" to a bell suspended in the air when "a light sprinkle of snow, falling upon it, is enough to make it vibrate." We find this same image in the verses above. An ancient Chinese commentary says, "When frost falls, the bells ring."[6] But here the image is of remarkable poetic density, for this ringing bell could be real (take special note of the reference in the last line to autumn, the season of frost, as well as the proximity of the monastery implied by the monk's presence). At the same time, however, the bell is metaphoric; that is, it is also possible to understand, it seems to me, that the "lingering tones" of the melody "enter" "the traveler's heart," which is washed clean of life's stains. Note the parallelism between this and the preceding line: the listener's consciousness, subtly engaged by the music, begins then to sound inwardly, not unlike the bell lightly weighed upon by a bit of frost.[7] Enchanted by the prolonged lingering of the music, the poet no longer heeds the arrival of evening. At last, the "beyond" of the sound gives rise to a "beyond" of the landscape: just as the sound continues on, so the landscape darkens and becomes opaque. The layering of piled-up clouds deepens the immensity of the darkened sky.

Considered in suitable musical terms, the softening of the timbre and the generous spacing of the measures that create this blandness. Having recalled the aesthetic of lingering tones dear to ancient ritual (loosened strings, the body of the instrument left unassembled, no accompanying orchestra . . .), another poet, Bo Juyi, pays homage to such music: "The melody is bland, rhythm spare, and sounds are few."[8] Or, elsewhere:

The cadence, slow; and leisurely the strumming:
Deep in the night, a few sounds, no more.
Bland, without flavor, they enter the ear;
The heart is tranquil, feelings lie beneath.[9]

It matters little whether or not the player goes on playing, the final couplet tells us, for one plays only for oneself and not for others; and the blandness of the sound entering the ear has already stirred a wealth of emotions. If the heart rejoices in this moment of tranquillity, it is because the blandness of those last notes has freed it from a too-focused awareness and eliminated all oppositions and contrasts:

The heart at rest — bland sounds:
There is no past or present.[10]

The blandness of sounds — a mind detached. This mind detaches itself not merely from the tumult of the world, or from external attachments, but from the grip of the music itself, to the extent that this latter implies feeling and tension. Blandness creates distance, diminishes the affective capacity, strips down our impressions to what is essential:

> The moon rises, birds nest, it is done;
> Silently sitting in an empty forest.
> At this moment, the world of mind is tranquil,
> And I can play my unadorned zither.
> Clarity and cold emerge from the nature of the woods,
> Calm and detachment in tune with man's heart . . .
> The sound lingers on, movement stops;
> The melody ends: an autumn night deepens.[11]

What "ends": the innumerable movements of the world, including this very tune now being played. What lasts (and unfolds): the sound that has been filtered, purified of itself, and the meditation it now inspires. And in the space across which music becomes silence, blandness sits at the threshold of that inner deepening, and calls us to the discovery of night.

CHAPTER TEN

Blandness's Change

of Signs in Literature

While poetry seems to have lent itself readily enough to a subtle celebration of musical blandness, recognition of a type of blandness specific to literature was longer in appearing. Only gradually, and in negative terms at first, did blandness take its place as a desired quality of poetry. It is, therefore, worthwhile to sketch out a history of this term in Chinese literary criticism insofar as this history itself, combined with the evolution of Chinese poetry, led to a reversal: the emerging possibility of a positive reading of blandness will serve to illuminate the lengthy maturation process of an aesthetic awareness.

When a writer of the Han dynasty, Wang Chong (first century C.E.), attempted to justify the rather unrefined character of his prose, the bland, insipid quality in question was judged a flaw.[1] Even more representative of this period is that when readers began to refer, in relation to literature, to the "lingering sound" associated with the spare and solemn music of vermilion strings, or to the "lingering flavor" of the unseasoned broth offered during the great ritual sacrifice, they seemed to lose sight of the common basis of these qualities. Indeed, they invoked them only when attempting to account for some literary imperfection. It is no coincidence that the first important writing on poetics in the

Chinese tradition, Lu Ji's "Wen fu" (Poetic exposition on literature), evaluates this deficiency as follows, placing it at the end of
a series of potential flaws:

> Or if [your expression] is pure and empty, and elegantly
>   contained;
> And you've eliminated all that is complicated or tends toward
>   overflowing —
> This is what will yield the left-over flavor of the great
>   ceremonial broth,
> And what will resemble the limpid tones shed by vermilion
>   cords:
> Even if it is true that "one sings alone and three join in
>   harmony,"
> Such [writing] may well be solemn and noble, but it will lack
>   charm.[2]

An obvious and seductive "charm" (*yan*), not the ephemeral,
limpid impression of emptiness (*qingxu*), is the supreme quality
sought in literature when it begins to grow conscious of itself, in
the third and fourth centuries. This period places particular value
on the decorative aspect of language, which it exploits beautifully,
and so the aesthetic dimension of literature takes center stage (so
much so that later critics would condemn their taste as "aestheticizing"). In fact, the limpidity of emptiness would only come to be
represented in a contemporaneous poetic mode during the reign
of the Yongjia from 307 to 311 that was developed by writers who,
passionate for the brand of philosophical Daoism that reemerges
during this time (just when Buddhism begins to make its way
through China as well), wrote poetry based more on reason than
on emotion. A later judgment would confirm as much: "During
the Yongjia period, there was considerable interest in the Daoist

tradition and esteem for 'pure talk.'[3] In the literature of this period, abstract thought was favored over lyric expression, and so literature was bland and without flavor."[4] In another example [drawn from the same text], a poet is praised for having "begun to transform the flat and bland style of the Yongjia period."[5] Plainness and blandness are thus still held to be negative values. But we also observe in these writings the seeds of the change that would soon follow: the imminent moment when poets would no longer treat emptiness and limpidity as subjects for discussion, and would cease formulating their intuition in clichéd aphorisms and metaphysical expressions, but would begin expressing that limpidity in emotion-rich landscapes. It is then that poetry is called on to capture the invisible by means of the perceptible, to evoke emptiness through the use of images. And it is from this time, too, that blandness would be less likely to connote the strict aridity of abstract meaning and would become more closely associated with an *atmosphere* imbuing the poem as a whole: the feeling for a necessary overcoming of the materiality of things, the experience of meaning that is never emphatic, but is elusive — always retreating further into the distance.

At the very heart of this critical discourse, the ever-increasing appreciation of "flavor" (*wei*) would in time transform blandness from a flaw into a positive quality.[6] In the major works of literary criticism, references to flavor are quite common and display two principal characteristics. First, literary flavor is most often conceived of in relation to the authenticity of feeling.[7] In particular, it is associated with the poetic evocation and consequent "symbolization" (*xing*) of a feature of the landscape seized on by the emotions.[8] Second, literary flavor is most appreciated for a quality that is as intangible as it is inexhaustible; it "flies" unceasingly "in all directions," as light and diffuse as the wind. And, like the wind, it envelops us without being seen:

When it is deep, the writing is both implicit and rich:
A lingering flavor enrobes it completely.[9]

With this, we see "lingering flavor" begin to take on literary significance. This quality allows the reader to "savor without growing weary" of the taste; our experience of this flavor "is without limit."[10] Emotional depth, imponderability, and infinite unfolding: the appreciation of taste naturally leads us toward the appreciation of blandness.

Thus it can hardly be deemed a revolution — or even a major change — when, during the Tang dynasty, the positive use of the term "blandness" (*dan*) makes its way into critical discourse. At the beginning, the term was merely used to qualify one style among many, with no indication of a particular preference. The following passage may well be the first to explicitly mention blandness as a positive quality of poetry (under the rubric "bland and common," or *dansu*):

> This manner [of writing] is like Xia Ji, [the young girl] behind the counter of the inn. She appears to be depraved but is, in fact, chaste. Here, the styles of Wu and Chu have been adopted. Although the style is common, it is not lacking in righteousness. As the ancient poem says:
>
> At the summit of Huayin Mountain,
> There is a well one hundred feet deep.
> Beneath it runs a spring
> So cold that it pierces to the bone.
> How sweet the young girl,
> Who has just gazed at her image in its waters!
> Nothing is reflected there,
> Except for the curve of her throat.[11]

In the Chinese tradition, poetry criticism is often a poetic undertaking itself, reveling in allusive, even cryptic expression. Rather
than reconstructing meaning through paraphrase, it tends to stim-
ulate one's receptivity in a broader sense. In this spirit, the first
image in the passage above is a negative one, presented only to
be surpassed: the young girl behind the counter at the inn (Sima
Xiangru's wife?) may at first make a bad impression.[12] But we are
given to believe in her inner righteousness, her hidden virtue. In
the same way, the love poems written in the style of Wu may
appear to be facile and quite "common," but at their core they are
no less engaging — or elusive — than the young girl gazing at her
reflection. One might also similarly construe the well dug into
the summit of the mountain. The water contained in its depths is
not directly visible; likewise, the young girl's reflection on the
water's surface, where "the curve of her throat" is all that appears
to the eye. Signs of restraint, discreet presence, and hidden
depths.

There is little doubt that the evolution of Chinese poetry itself
is what provoked the recognition of the virtues of such blandness.
The figure of the poet Tao Yuanming playing his stringless zither
had already marked the start of a new tradition. Then, during the
Tang, several great poets (such as Wang Wei, Wei Yingwu, and
Liu Zongyuan) continued in this vein. Critical reflection came
later. The following poem, "Chongdan" (Harmony-Blandness),
composed at the end of the Tang, was written precisely in praise
of blandness:

> Given over, by its nature, to silence,
> It is one with the secret of things.
> It quaffs of the Supreme Harmony;
> Then, alone, with the goose, it takes flight.

Like the spring breeze
That lightly brushes his robes:
Sound — sensed through the bamboo,
The beauty that one then takes away as it returns.

You meet it, without going deep.
Search for it, and it grows ever more tenuous.
If, at last, it does take on form,
You've barely grasped its hand, and already it is gone.[13]

Here, the presentation of the theme is more consistent than in the preceding poem and is developed in three stages. The first lines evoke the existential and metaphysical basis (to describe them in terms familiar to Western readers) of this type of poetic experience. Simplicity, silence, and indifference open the way to the intimate workings of nature and bring mind into step with reality in its most subtle state (ll. 1–2): harmony is apprehended at its source, that is, at a stage preceding its actualization as a phenomenon and in inverse relation to its development as such. This elevation of mind is linked with a certain detachment regarding the everyday world, now perceived as too common (ll. 3–4). In the second stage, the poem depicts how blandness comes about: its manifestation is subtle, indirect, never substantiated. In lines 5–8, the spring breeze does not pass through the clothing, but suffuses it gently, imperceptibly; the sound does not strike the ear directly, but is transmitted through a veil of bamboo: muffled, filtered, and thus revealed. One does not just hear it; one senses it within. This beauty that is blandness's is not something to be fixed, isolated, and possessed; instead, it is carried (conveyed) through the life force of all things and can only be experienced in its entirety, by distancing oneself from individuations or approaching them only at the moment when they begin to emerge from their transitory existence, when they are engaged on the path of return (l. 8).

Now the problem is apparent: How can harmony, rooted in the invisible, express itself in concrete terms — in a perceptible mode — by way of signs? In this contradiction, the intangible nature of blandness is born, for it appears only at the very edges of the perceptible, at the portal of the Invisible. If it lends itself to concrete manifestation, it is only in order to lead us away: to the harmonious transcending, the silent resolution, of such manifestations. This brings us to the importance of the Daoist-inspired motif of "return," appearing at the end of the second part of the poem. The bland does not utter the things of the world — does not paint the world — except at their point of assimilation back into the Undifferentiated, where they shed their distinctive traits, integrate their differences, and give reign to their propensity for fusion. An imponderable quality (this quality of the imponderable!), blandness is, of necessity, fugitive, as suggested in the concluding stanza of the poem (ll. 9–12). It evades all who would pursue it through methodical, intentional searching; you will not grasp its hand in order to keep it with you.

We have already seen that Chinese criticism never allows for the separation between a literary style and its corresponding state of consciousness: while the dimension of the blandness of things subverts all effort and escapes our grasp, it nevertheless will surrender itself, on its own, to one whose spirit has attained a state of openness by ridding itself of all attachments and intentionality. It is thus that the underlying foundation for the spontaneous and unmotivated transpiring of poetic language is recovered in all its intensity and sensitivity. There would be little point in invoking irrationality or calling on the mythology of poetic inspiration to illuminate this process: the very nature and exigencies of blandness suffice to account for these conditions of poetic possibility.

I have refrained thus far, even in my discussion of literary "theory," from referring to blandness as a concept. This is because, in general, Chinese criticism does not function on the basis of concepts and does not operate from the perspective of analytic knowledge. But it does speak of literature in terms of value and, with an eye to improving one's ability to appreciate it, illuminates it from the perspective of polarities and webs of affinity. This is evident even in the title of the above poem: "Chongdan," or "Harmony-Blandness" (or "detachment"). The title is not a single, complete expression that can be disposed of by simply taking stock of its content but a balance between two terms that together make up a binomial in which each element simultaneously attracts and complements the other. (This principle is at work throughout: the titles of the twenty-four poems dedicated to representing twenty-four poetic modes — of which the present poem on bland-ness is number two — are all conceived along the same lines.) At the same time that a given binomial expression represents a cer-tain internal balance, it also represents an analogous equilibrium with the poetic modes that immediately precede and follow it. In this, we find a notable theoretical rigor, though quite different from Western modes of theorizing. It culminates in a construct that is as efficient as it is subtle: each poetic mode simultaneously complements and extends the preceding one, creating a move-ment from one mode to the next that both preserves and renews the "center."

It is worth looking more closely at this continuous reestablish-ment of equilibrium (analogous to the regulating process of the cosmic Dao), for it provides the clearest path — clearer than any conceptual analysis — to understanding harmony. We find "Har-mony-Blandness" situated between "Force-Incipiency" (*xionghun*) and "Delicacy-Luxuriance" (*xiannong*). As explained by the com-mentator, if *xiong*, or "force," grows too strong, it becomes vio-lence; and if *hun*, or "undifferentiation" (the defining quality of origins), is taken too far, it becomes adulterated, impure — which brings us to blandness. But the same holds true, then, for "Harmony-Blandness": if harmony reaches an extreme, it culminates in total indifference, and, by virtue of the element of blandness, it could become monotonous and boring, which would then naturally lead to the next poetic mode in which delicacy and luxuriance attract the eye and stir the spirit once more. Far from being a concept, blandness represents a balance, an intermediate moment, a transitory stage constantly threatened with obliteration.

Transitory between two poles: on the one side, a too-tangible, sterile, and limited manifestation; on the other, an overly volatile evanescence, where everything disappears and is forgotten. Caught between the dangers of signifying too much and of ceasing to function as a sign at all, the bland sign is just barely one. It consists not of the absence of signs but of a sign that is in the process of emptying itself of its signifying function, on the verge of becoming absent: as marks of an invisible harmony, or scattered traces.

This is also why, following the same principle of the balancing of poetic values, blandness is not merely one poetic mode among twenty-four, but, as the perceptible expression of harmony, cuts across them all and links them together. And so even in his treatment of a poetic mode like "Shimmer-Beauty" (*qili*), the author observes:

> Things rich in color run out, dry up,
> While things that are bland grow gradually richer.[14]

Blandness, prompting one to gradual and never-ending discovery, is the richest of the poetic modes. As such, it flows free from all attempts to master it and can be neither contained nor "gathered," as suggested in the poem "Limpid-Sublime" (*qingqi*):

93

> The spirit that emanates from ancient distinctiveness:
> So bland that it cannot be gathered. [15]

Once again, the blandness of signs refers us back to the mind's capacity for detachment. Concerning "Classical-Elegant" (*dianya*):

> Petals fall — not a word.
> The man is bland-detached: like the chrysanthemums.[16]

Blandness should be pictured not from a specific point of view (be it stylistic, psychological, or moral) but globally; it is itself a "world" that must be entered. Its season is late autumn, when chrysanthemum petals are falling, touched by frost: the last colors of the year are fading, an erasing that happens on its own, in simple withdrawal. One who has attained a calm and meditative state will understand the inescapable logic of decline and will refrain from weighing it down with superfluous meanings or sentimental utterances. "When you understand without the aid of a word or a sentence, the flavor will last all the longer," notes a commentator in reference to these two lines of poetry. Any word is one too many, adding nothing but superfluity, a futile flailing of the arms. The only comment to which blandness might lend itself is a brusque and simple "no comment."

94

CHAPTER ELEVEN

The Ideology of Blandness

The ultimate stage of its development: the beginning of the Song dynasty in the eleventh century. Blandness is now openly acknowledged as an ideal in the creation of poetry:

> In composing a poem, in the present as in the past,
> Only the creation of the plain and bland is hard.[1]

It is by now understood that this plainness "extends into the depths" and that this blandness harbors "plenitude" (*pingdan suimei*).[2] Once joined in this way, *ping* and *dan* — "plainness" and "blandness" — will henceforth constitute a category commonly raised in poetic treatises.[3] In addition, there is the awareness that blandness in this sense can only be attained after a period of development — that it is the fruit of a certain maturity. Such is the case, for example, for specific individuals. One great poet of the Tang dynasty, Du Fu, is characterized as having been "brilliant and flowering" in his youth, only to become, later in life, "plain and bland."[4] After the vigorous dynamism of youth, when a host of newly acquired strengths vie to express themselves, there comes the time when those strengths settle down and direct themselves inward. That this blandness comes *afterward*, through the supersession of one's earlier exuberance, ensures its plenitude and distinguishes the bland definitively from the "facile" and the "erratic," with which it might otherwise be confused.[5] And this holds true for the overall development of literary history as well: "All literatures start out brilliant and flowering, only to become, later on, plain and bland." This later period is, then, their "autumn" and their "winter."[6] The time of blandness is thus delineated by nature; the cycle of the seasons, the logic of which plays an important role in Chinese thought, serves to justify this final phase of the dissolution of abundance and inward retraction.

As widespread as this acknowledgment of the poetic bland had become, a certain ambiguity continued to characterize its ideological implications. This is largely because it operated on two different levels simultaneously — sometimes within the writing of a single author, or even in a single sentence. While it is true that the two levels shared a common intuitive basis, their orientations and applications were quite distinct.

The first draws its inspiration from the Confucian tradition and even assumes a rather vehement stance, common in the early Song, against the supposed disintegration of the Chinese tradition provoked by the heterodox trends of Daoism and Buddhism. As one poet [Ouyang Xiu] wrote about the poetry of another [Mei Yaochen]:

> Its expression is chaste, its meaning honorable, basic but not banal;
> Its ancient flavor, while bland, is not feeble.[7]

There is little question that this interpretation of blandness appears to us in the West as the least appealing, accustomed as we are today to separating morality from aesthetics. Nevertheless, I would like to explore the logic underlying this intuition, if only because doing so will allow us to raise questions concerning our own view (the heritage of Romanticism, inculcated in us by our own modernity, and which we apply naturally), leading us to ask whether our truest feelings — those most deeply rooted in ourselves — might not also necessarily be good (as suggested by Mencius). According to the Chinese tradition, these "good feelings" give rise to "good literature" (and here I reformulate, by inversion, André Gide's assertion[8]). The "righteousness" (zheng) raised in the above passage does not only involve condemning ideological heterodoxy and embracing the virtues of consistency and effort (as the only ones that allow man to rise to a higher moral level). It also harbors an affective dimension: one that, far from clashing with our contemporary sensibilities (as an externally imposed exigency), opens us up to the depths of the world and inspires us to be touched by what is essential. This is why it can inspire the writing of poetry.

But here a more comprehensive explanation (one more anthropological in nature) is in order. Indeed, how are we to understand this moral dimension of emotion and its power over us — that is, its artistic value? In the context of classical Chinese thought, emotions are a "response" (gan) to some stimulus in the world that stirs us (dong). The profundity of emotion increases in direct proportion to the significance of the external stimulus. At the same time, the deeper the emotion, the less it can be considered individual — the less limited it is to our own personal (egocentric) concerns — and, conversely, the greater its capacity to awaken us to the richness of our link with the world and to the degree of our involvement in the great process of things. It is thus that it opens our subjectivity onto the unity of all beings, the interdependence of diverse realities, and draws it out of its particular — exclusive and limited — viewpoint. Because of this intensity, it is able to make us connect across the real and raise us to the level of a

97

shared, fundamentally human perspective (as suggested by the Confucian value *ren*, or humanity). And so the deeper the emotion, the stronger its moral tenor and the greater its capacity to stir others deeply as well, unconstrained by the limits of a specific object or concern. The moral function of emotion, then, does not limit emotion's significance or its potential (as we find in our own moralizing and didactic poetry). Quite the opposite: by anchoring emotion more solidly (that is, by putting it in closer touch, through our perception, with the foundation of things and of life), the moral function develops it all the more fully — indeed, to an infinite extent. And the *scope* of this significance accounts for its beauty.

As for the reference to the "ancient," it is meant to bring to mind a sobriety associated with the classical period and conveys both a rejection of the complaisance of rhetorical flourish and a graver and more basic view of literature. Here literature is not practiced for the pure pleasure of art but bears the responsibility for man's moral elevation and thus plays an important role in the ordering of the world. In this context, allusion to the unseasoned broth of ancient ritual seems unavoidable:

> The blandness of the ancients harbors true flavor:
> What need is there to season the great broth?[9]

This trueness, this "authenticity" (*zhen*), with its moral connotations, pertains to the expression of our basic nature. When, in refusing superficial enticements, we keep ourselves from slipping into partiality and from undertaking projects both too local and too limited (to preserve, that is, the value of centrality), we also preserve the fresh spontaneity of our ability to respond to the totality of the real — in all its incommensurability. And this capacity renders our engagement in the world authentic and enables us to stay connected to the universe as a whole. From a subjective standpoint, blandness is also beneficial in that it foils the expectations of false desires, demands us to give up our crude and facile satisfactions, and requires us to extend our concerns beyond the immediate confines of our existence. In short, it leads us to surpass our limits, and in doing so, it becomes a wellspring of hard work by goading us to exert ourselves:

> Of late, his poems have taken on a certain ancient stringency,
> Harsh and hard to chew;
> It is, at first, like eating olives,
> Whose flavor grows more pronounced with time.[10]

Stringency and harshness: this motif of a preliminary (beneficial) frustration, of a deliberately disappointing first encounter (which incites us to pursue our search even further), is pushed to that paradoxical point where blandness starts to "sting." The poet thus described replies in like terms:

> I compose my verses in keeping with my basic nature,
> Attempting to attain the plain and bland.
> My words are harsh: neither rounded nor softened,
> And sting the mouth even more than water chestnuts or lotus
>   seeds.[11]

And so savoring poetic blandness becomes an exercise in asceticism: as a result of the effort required to "chew" and the necessity of extended salivating, easily accessible flavors and false beauty are all abandoned in exchange for more fundamental values. At the beginning of the Song dynasty, there is, in effect, a purposeful reaction against excessive formal refinement and the pleasures afforded by the stunningly odd, studied effect — pleasures that had

emerged as a poetic temptation at the end of the Tang and per-
sisted up to this period. This is why poetry now took on qualities
of the rough and unadorned — "neither rounded nor softened" —
and, in striving to rid itself of false allure, moved closer to the
genre of prose writing. But there is more to this trend than the
simple reaction of one style against another. Through the blandness and plainness of a more forbidding, less alluring poetic writing — one that "stings" us by violating our aestheticizing taste —
we gradually discover the taste of the neutral, which reveals, as
we have learned, the basic virtues of balance and centrality, the
fundamental characteristics of nature's regular pattern of alternation, of the wordless process of the real. Blandness is not merely a
path to inner cultivation; it is also the "principle of things":

> Poetry in its essence gives voice to our affective nature;
> There is little point in shouting so loud!
> Once you realize that the principle of things consists of the
>   plain and bland,
> From dawn to dusk, you will find yourself in the Unending
>   Light.[12]

The expression "Unending Light" (*yuanming*) is a play on the
name of Tao Yuanming, the poet of simplicity frequently mentioned in another context. The reference here is ambiguous and
makes it possible to interpret the connotation of the poetics of
blandness somewhat differently from before: as suggesting a certain distance from social obligations and worldly cares, as occurs
when the mind frees itself from all constraints and recovers its
spontaneity. Here the Daoist or Buddhist connotations inform its
expression. Of one poet, it was said that his poetry is "bland and
tranquil, detached and remote" (*danbo xianyuan*); and of another
poet [Mei Yaochen, mentioned above], that this "plain and bland"

poetry is "limpid and lovely, detached and unfettered" (*qingli xiansi pingdan*).[13] And this poet, in turn, said the following about another friend:

> The poetry he writes when his spirit joins with the flow of things and takes joy in his own feelings is plain and bland, profound and complete: one forgets, as one reads it, all worldly cares. His writing achieves the utmost in tranquillity and correctness, and never criticizes his subject. It is thus that one becomes aware that his taste is broad and far-reaching and that he expresses his harmonious relation with the world through his poetry.[14]

This line of thinking about poetic blandness would prove particularly fruitful with time. True, the two perspectives find common ground in their equal attachment to simplicity and in the fundamental importance they accord to the principle of harmony (concerning which all schools of thought seem to agree). And as the tradition develops, despite a certain will toward orthodoxy, syncretism — another manifestation of harmony — tends to dominate, albeit unconsciously. But it remains true that this act of *transcending* — of detachment — enjoined by the poetic bland can be conceived in two different ways: either in terms of its progression, which implies durative time and targets the disappointment inherent in superficial pleasures; or in terms of its connection with the emptiness of things, where it signifies the freeing from consciousness and its attainment of perfect openness. If we were to resort to the use of familiar labels (even knowing that we thus run the risk of oversimplifying the distinction), we might refer to the one dimension as more moralistic and the other as more mystical — blandness as incarnating the value of either *effort* or *ecstasy*. But the intuitive notion of the bland tends to resist being inserted into abstract categories such as these. That is why it has been largely expressed in poetic and imagistic language. So, opposite the *olive* that must be patiently and insistently chewed before surrendering its flavor, let us propose the perfectly limpid flavor of *water.*

Chapter Twelve

Flavor-Beyond-the-Flavorful,

Landscape-Beyond-Landscapes

The motif of literary flavor never retreats into the isolation of mere metaphor, never loses contact with its primary referent of the sense of taste — and it is here that we find its main interest. Reading and eating, as conceived in Chinese thought, are linked by something more than just analogy. The reader of a poem is engaged not so much in an act of decoding meaning (following our intellectualized view) as in incorporating a substance (the words of the text) that, having started out as exterior to him, then exerts its influence through him in a process of slow and gradual infiltration (one is reminded of the Chinese expression *tiwei*). This is why Chinese poetic criticism so often seems disappointing to us, dispensing as it does with textual analysis, with working through the text as form or model, and counting instead on the effect of our assimilation of it: the reader is simply advised to "intone" the poem many times, to "repeat" it in the mouth, to "chew" it in silence.[1] And this is also why the motif of literary flavor does not in the least aspire to the elaboration of a typology (as we find in the taxonomy of the Sanskrit *rasa*). Its significance, rather, when brought to bear on our own practice, is of a more phenomenological order: to illuminate as directly (and thus as comprehensively) as possible how consciousness experiences the full exercise of the senses, and to identify the most favorable conditions for doing so.

This experience common to both reading and eating goes even further, for the logic of pleasure is also one and the same: it depends on the logic of retention. And this stands in direct opposition to the usual tendency toward consumption. Their common basis is apparent in the following letter, which marks the beginning of a theoretical interpretation of blandness as a poetics of the invisible and the detached ("Letter on Poetry" by Sikong Tu):

> In the region south of Jiangling [that is, outside the realm of Chinese cultural dominance], people are generally content to enjoy the pleasurable aspects of food, and that's all. In the case of vinegar, which is, of course, sour, they go no further than its sourness; in the case of brine, which is, of course, very salty, they go no further than its saltiness. In contrast, true Chinese stop themselves from continuing to eat as soon as their hunger has been sated; they understand that [if they continue] they would then pass up a certain kind of plenitude that lies beyond the sour and the salty. (As for the people of Jiangling, as we might suspect, they are used to doing things their way and do not perceive this distinction.)[2]

What detracts from strong flavors such as brine or vinegar is that they are fully encompassed by their identification as distinct flavors — the salty and the sour, respectively — rather than evolving into something beyond themselves. The southerners, nevertheless, remain forever attached to the immediate intensity of flavor and allow themselves to be limited by it. But the art of savoring lies in knowing when to stop in order to allow other flavor notes to reveal themselves. In this context, then, the traditional expression "discerning flavors" takes on a relatively new meaning. It is a matter not so much of discerning among the various flavors (such as salty or sour) as of recognizing within one particular flavor the distinction between the fundamental (dense and opaque) taste that first imposes itself as such and its "beyond," which becomes apparent as it lingers — expanding, purified of the first shock to the senses, which is ultimately just that and nothing more. In itself, contact with the flavor represents only the zero degree of the true experience of it, an experience that becomes all the richer for its development through its relative absence (in one's stopping eating). This, in turn, serves as an ideal for poetic writing:

> When it is close at hand without being superficial, and when it is far-reaching without knowing any boundaries — only then can we speak of the excellence of beyond-resonance.[3]

According to the late–Tang dynasty author of this letter (Sikong Tu, the author of the poem "Harmony-Blandness" that we read earlier), the most able practitioners of this poetics (Wang Wei and Wei Yingwu) express themselves in a manner that is "limpid and bland, refined and pure" (*chengdan jingzhi*) and in this way possess their own distinct and rigorous styles.[4] As for their flavor, the author says elsewhere, it is "limpid, extending into the distance like a wind that only grows stronger as it gusts from peak to peak" (or, following a textual variant, "like limpid water that spreads across [the ground]").[5] Furthermore, the poetic form that best corresponds to such an expansion of flavor is, logically, the one that stops "saying" soonest — that is, the shortest form, the quatrain.

> The composition of the quatrain presupposes the most finely honed abilities, for all of the variations and transformations it sets in motion operate under a spiritual process that is spontaneous and beyond our ken.[6]

Just as true flavor only becomes manifest somewhere beyond our sensual and immediate contact with food, poetic joy can only be felt in going beyond the linguistic substance of the poem or, as the Chinese say, in the realm "beyond words." As one would expect, the exercise of the senses is all the richer when verbal substance is restrained (as in the twenty syllables allotted to the *jueju*, or five-character quatrain). Blandness is the poetic quality that opens the way to this unceasing *transformation*.

Chinese critics have commented on the following quatrain in terms of its poetic blandness (in this case, I have preferred to render the text word by word, leaving the translation to the reader):

> mountain — empty / not — notice — person
> only — hear / of man — voice — echo
> return — ray / penetrate — depths — forest
> again — shine / green — moss — above[7]

As described by one commentator on this poem, "poetry values the transmission of meaning, and the transmission of meaning values what is far and not what is close by, what is bland and not what is pronounced: that which is remarkable and close by is easy to know, whereas it is difficult to recognize that which is bland and far away."[8] For this traditional Chinese critic, indicating the presence of blandness suffices to open the way for the reader's interpretation, and he refuses to impose any further commentary (except to give other examples). We find the same judgment in the writings of a modern critic: "Although bland, the poem's expression is redolent with meaning."[9]

Looking more closely at the poem, we notice that the entire quatrain develops in an atmosphere of presence and absence, of manifestation and retreat. For example, the topos of solitude, introduced in the first verse, is counterbalanced in the second by the echoes of someone's voice. Rather than expanding on this topos through its rhetorical amplification or thematic elaboration, the poem holds back from any type of obvious, too-emphatic exposition: the speaker is alone but not cut off from others; the mountain is empty yet still reveals traces of human presence. A theme is roughed out, but only in a limited way; some distance has been taken, but it is only relative. This solitude is neither grandiloquent in its expression nor ascetic in its intention, for it is in stopping at the threshold of solitude (as the poet stops at the threshold of this theme) that one becomes most alive to its virtual dimension and that one feels its allure most deeply. "Mountain" and "man": the mind remains open to both possibilities, enjoying each through the other, never giving itself over to worldly cares or obliterating itself in nothingness.

These first two lines recall those of Tao Yuanming, the first great poet of the bland:

I built my hut in the world of men,
But never heard cart nor horse.[10]

They also subtly invert their meaning. In the verses of this earlier poet, we find (to use the Chinese expression) "solitude in the midst of noise"; in those of Wang Wei, the poet Tao inspired, we find "noise in the midst of solitude."

Evidence of this art of balancing (from which blandness is born) is present even in the poem's structure: between the intercourse of the natural with the human world (ll. 1–2) and the interactions that take place within the natural world (ll. 3–4). And it appears, too, in thematic reversals: when a ray of sunlight illumines the darkness (l. 3), and the shade thus produced reflects back the light (l. 4); and when the movement of penetration (into the depths of the forest) is counterbalanced with that of shining on the surface of the moss.

One could trace in even greater detail the harmonizing play of concurrent tensions, of polarities that eventually neutralize each other. "Only" — the first word of the second line — attenuates the meaning of the first line; the faculty of hearing is balanced against visual perception; verbal articulation acts to "positivize" the preceding negation; "return" and "again," placed in parallel positions at the beginning of the last two lines (the rays of the setting sun against the reflection of its light on the moss), together form a running binomial that signifies departure and return, the unceasing coming and going of things.

Poetic blandness depends, then, on our senses' never leaning markedly in one direction or another; rather, the senses must allow phenomena and situations to appear without interference. Nothing overwhelms the attention, nothing else is obscured by its presence, and things no sooner emerge than they retreat and change. As formulated in a beautiful Chinese expression of Buddhist inspiration, consciousness neither "attaches" itself to things nor "separates" itself from them (*buji buli*); it neither clings to the realism of phenomena, losing itself in their midst, nor breaks with them absolutely, to retreat into a vision (just as illusory and forced) of a noumenal void, where it would risk depriving itself of their renewal, their fresh recurrence. Instead, the distance at which consciousness has placed things should remain allusive, and the relative non-differentiation of these phenomena should nevertheless remain positive, ready for the longest of inward journeys.

This endless exhalation of the senses, this giving off of a subtle, harmoniously diffuse flavor (which is, therefore, all the more present to consciousness), is rendered in this lovely image: "The language [literally, the scenes evoked by their language — TRANS.] of the poets resembles what is produced when, in the Azure Fields beneath the warmth of the sun, a hidden piece of jade emanates a vapor: one can contemplate it, but one cannot fix it precisely with one's gaze." Such are "representation-beyond-representation" and "landscape-beyond-landscape" (*xiangwai zhi xiang, jingwai zhi jing*).[11]

These images, these expressions, come together as sufficient, comprehensible references to a tradition. Self-contained, surrounded by silence, they possess the allure of the perfect formulation. It is thus necessary to make the effort to disturb this formulaic perfection and, taking it as a starting point, regenerate inquiry: How do we understand this "beyond" (of flavor or of landscape)? One would like to see a more precise interpretation — from a poetic point of view — of the capacity for "remote" expansion and diffusion facilitated by blandness. Another famous letter [by Su Dongpo], written two centuries later, takes on this same line of questioning but shifts it to the more easily accessible (because more directly perceptible) subject of the graphic line; here, for once, brush writing serves as metaphor for that other type of writing — poetry. And the illustrative value of the parallel is called into play as well: the author begins by contrasting two periods in the development of Chinese calligraphy, the masters of the fourth century and those of the Tang:

> Regarding calligraphy, I consider the written traces left by Zhong You and Wang Xizhi to be desolate-spare-simple-remote, and that the marvel of their achievement lies beyond the line and the brush. During the Tang, Yan Zhenqing and Liu Gongquan began to synthesize all of the techniques — ancient and modern — for handling the brush, and they deployed those techniques fully, exploiting to the utmost the many possibilities of calligraphy. They are recognized as

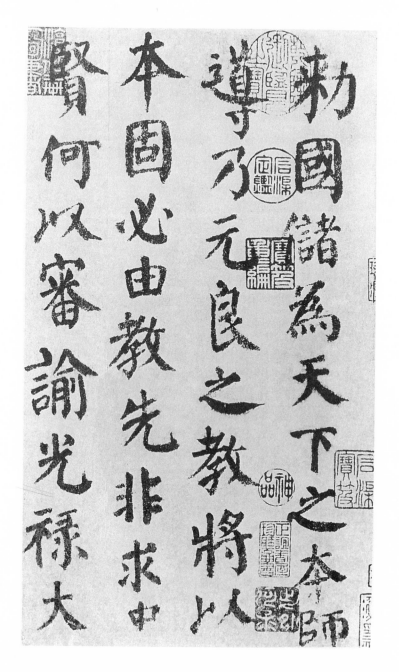

Figure 12.1. An example of "perfectly achieved" calligraphy. Beginning fragment of a "handscripted certificate" by Yan Zhenqing, 8th century.

Figure 12.2. An example of more "remote" and ephemeral calligraphy, evocative of blandness. "Letter to an Aunt" by Wang Xizhi, 4th century (here, the same name as the calligrapher).

masters by one and all; but the art of Zhong and Wang was of a greater subtlety.[12]

It has become common in China to compare the different arts through analogy and to articulate the requirements of one through a description of the other. Just like the great calligraphic masters of the Tang who knew how to benefit from tradition and who pushed their own virtuosity to the extreme, the Tang poets Li Bo and Du Fu are considered the "greatest" poets — those who have most completely mastered their art:

> By virtue of the brilliance of their talent, they surpass all other gen-
> erations and excel over all poets past and present. But at the same
> time, that air of having risen above the world of dust, which we find
> [earlier] in the poetry of the Wei and Jin, is ever so slightly lost.[13]

Something here is worth thinking about: the most accomplished work of art is not necessarily the most effective; indeed, by virtue of its very perfection it is found lacking. If the calligraphy of the great masters of the Tang is the most accomplished, it must nev-ertheless surrender its supreme position, at least from a certain point of view, to that of the preceding period, a period that was profoundly simple, whose characters appeared on the page as most spare and scant, as if they had simply been left there, aban-doned by the brush, rather than as the fruit of concentrated atten-tion, of the focused practice of an art (figures 14.1 and 14.2). Far from seeking to impose their dynamic rhythm on us, far from actively demonstrating qualities of consistency and vitality, they seem to have lost a bit of their density, to already be somewhat less than fully present, as if on the verge of taking their leave. It is as though they were taking care not to commit themselves to the world, consort with the real, or establish themselves too solidly (expressions that at first had served to characterize an air of superior detachment among individuals). These written characters are transitory vestiges of an inspiration come from somewhere else, which animates them from afar and of which they preserve a certain nostalgia: these written lines are perceived only as traces, and so exude an air of renunciation that surrounds calligraphy with a halo of indistinctness and solitude.

The same holds true for poetic writing. Pre-Tang poetry conveys a certain feeling of detachment — insofar as signs are perceived as evocations of one's inner state — that raises us above the "world of dust" (as described by the Buddhist expression *gao feng jue chen*), the world of perceptible characteristics and our investment in them. This quality of writing brings us back, as one would expect, to the sentiment of the bland:

> Although the poets who came after Li Bo and Du Fu might also at times possess the [same] distant resonance, their talent remains just this side of their ambitions. Only Wei Yingwu and Liu Zongyuan knew how to bring forth a delicate luxuriance in the heart of ancient simplicity and to project in blandness the most intense flavor.[14]

To give an example, the last two lines of the following poem have often been read in the spirit of "having risen above this world of dust":

> This morning the prefect's office is cold;
> Suddenly I think of a wanderer in the mountains:
> Is he gathering bracken at the base of the ravine
> So that he can boil his white stones when he returns home?
>
> I would like to take him a gourd of wine,
> To cheer him on this gloomy eve ...

But fallen leaves cover the empty mountains:
Could I find his traces there?[15]

Here — there; the town center — nature. A cold morning in the
office in town suddenly calls to mind the "wanderer" (ke) — literally, a "guest" (a guest of the mountain or, despite the distance
that separates them, of the poet?) — a monk who lives alone on
the mountain. The next two lines evoke the simple life of the
monk, for it is in the most banal tasks — "gathering bracken," for
example — rather than in the more ostentatious acts of piety that
the deepest spirituality resides (note that the "white stones"
allude to a Daoist monk of ancient times who, having run out of
provisions while on a voyage at sea, boiled stones for food). The
"gourd of wine" is another reminder of the simple life (borrowed
this time from the Confucian tradition[16]) even as it vividly renders
the feeling of austerity and remoteness. As usual, it is autumn.
The atmosphere, introduced with this evocation of purity, by the
end of the poem swells with the feeling of absence. All tangible
signs gesture toward their own relinquishing. In the next-to-last
line, then, the oxymoron of fullness and emptiness, which we
translate here word for word — "fill — empty — mountain" is not
merely a rhetorical ploy. Rather, it gives us to understand that the
fullness that acts as screen (by hiding the traces that would allow
the poet to join the recluse) is composed only of ephemeral realities, no sooner recognized than already emptied of substance: the
"leaves" that fall. And as for the final line of the poem, it echoes a
line written much earlier by that poet of the bland Tao Yuanming,
"Silence everywhere, no footprints," but it does so in a way that
intensifies the implicit movement toward erasure. Again, we do
well to adhere to a word-for-word translation, "where — to seek
— step — traces?," for then we see more clearly how the feeling of
absence is not presented abruptly or definitively. It makes itself

114

known gradually; we *become* aware of it. This is a function not only of the interrogative tenor of the phrase but also of the overall effect of graduated progression (described in a movement not toward an ever-more-emphatic presence but toward the removal of that presence). The reference to a place, appearing at the beginning of the line, loses its pertinence little by little and ultimately eludes us completely; this other life acquires an ideal dimension, even though we know that its only real *place* is internal. At the same time that the signs are emptied of substance, their "beyond" attracts us. And so the last line provides just such a figure of detachment.

This poem performs a type of conversion on its readers; but the "beyond" to which it invites us is not a metaphysical one. It is not a world separate from the one we have here, but the same one (the only one) cleansed of its opacity, liberated from its realism, and returned to its original state of freshness. This is why it is expressed as blandness and why poetry is its vehicle. And this vision would soon become an integral part of literary thought:

> Question: According to the ancients, one must acquire the ability to distinguish among flavors before beginning to be able to talk about poetry. Might I ask you on what basis one can distinguish among poetic flavors?
>
> Answer: According to Sikong Tu of the Tang, he who would begin to study poetry must recognize "the flavor that is beyond flavor," an expression often cited by Su Dongpo that has since had much currency. If one desires to study poems by those such as Tao Yuanming, Wang Wei, Wei Yingwu, or Liu Zongyuan, it behooves him to seek true flavor in the plain and bland. At first, one does not perceive it, but the longer one savors it, the more enduring its impression. It is similar to what occurred when Lu Hongjian tasted

the flavor of the water of different springs of the world, and he accorded first place to the waters of the great river of Zhongling. The flavor of its waters is bland but, in fact, it is not bland, it is the best flavor in the world, with which the flavor of no other food can compare. Naturally, "those who can appreciate the flavor of food" are already quite "rare," but those who can appreciate the flavor of water are even more so.[17]

We are witness here to the definitive acknowledgment of a poetic tradition. It is attested to in the reference to the same poets (forming a list, henceforth canonical, that would serve to denote it): Tao Yuanming, Wang Wei, Wei Yingwu, and Liu Zongyuan. And it avails itself of the same assertions: blandness contains the ultimate flavor; things at first unnoticed become more and more engaging until they become unforgettable; the ideal flavor is that of water.

Nevertheless, we must not forget what such a tradition preserves of its origins. Of course, we in the West have acquired the habit (a habit that finds support in the empire of linguistics) of conceptualizing signs as a function of independently operating systems unrelated to states of mind, emotions, or ideologies. This very habit made possible the establishment of an independent science known as semiotics. But as we have come to realize in reading the above poems, the (virtual) richness of the bland is inextricable from a particular insight regarding existence (that is, detachment regarding phenomena, a sense of the emptiness inherent in all things, and so on); this remoteness is accessible only through a certain inward journey, a journey facilitated by that same blandness. From this perspective, then, the bland sign does not fulfill the sign's "natural" role of representing; more to the point, it "de-represents," connoting a "beyond" that is not symbolic.

CHAPTER THIRTEEN

The "Margin" and the

"Center" of Flavor

It is also possible to invert our perspective: thus, the dimension of remoteness is no longer visualized as opening outward on the exterior world; rather, plenitude is situated within. The beyond of blandness is now the "center" (*zhong*) of flavor, and blandness itself is its "margin" (*bian*). The logic of transcending has not changed, but it is enriched by a new intuition of distinctly Buddhist inspiration. From this inverted perspective, then, we can more clearly perceive the distinction between the freeing effect of blandness and the tension inherent in the usual, more familiar symbolic relations:

> Liu Zongyuan's poems are inferior to those of Tao Yuanming but superior to those of Wei Yingwu. Han Yu's poems excel in their vigor of feeling and audacity of expression but are less successful in achieving a serene and reserved profundity. The reason why we value the dry and bland is that, if the outside is sere, the inside will be lush; and apparent blandness contains beauty. This is what we find in the poetry of Tao Yuanming or Liu Zongyuan. But if, in the center as at the margins, the whole were sere and bland, would it even be worth talking about? According to the Buddhists, "It is like eating honey. People find that it is completely sweet, in the center as at the margins." When

they taste the five flavors, people distinguish between the bitter and the sweet. But how rare are those who, in tasting one flavor, can distinguish between the "center" and the "margin."[1]

The outside is bland, but the inside is lush; one only need move from the disappointing margin of flavor to the plenitude contained in the center. Two lines at the end of a poem by the same author, Su Dongpo, reveal with even greater clarity what is meant here by "centrality":

Salty and sour, both are part of what we enjoy;
But the center harbors the supreme flavor, one that never
    fades away.[2]

Such, then, is the value of the center. We are already familiar with the importance accorded to centrality by Confucian thought: by keeping to the center, one avoids slipping into a position of partiality, which would block our innate capacity to evolve in harmony with the world. And so one reconnects with the neutrality that is essential to the great, wordless process of things — a neutrality from which flows the regularity and constancy of that process. In the Madhyamika (or Middle Way) school of Buddhism, appearing in India at the beginning of the Common Era, centrality's value is found in its relation to emptiness (*sunya*). The middle transcends the opposition between the bipolar extremes of existence and nonexistence, affirmation and negation, pleasure and pain. The middle ensures that truth is not dualistic. As long as truth remains relative and proceeds from human reasoning, then the distinctions between subject and object, between the false and the true, will persist. But once one has achieved a full understanding of emptiness and of the unreality of all phenomena, absolute truth (*prajna*) "contains nothing concrete or individual that can make it an object of particularization."[3] And it is precisely toward this understanding that the Chinese notion of the bland leads us.

When the Middle Way school of Buddhism made its way into China by incorporating some Daoist elements, it brought with it the model of rigorous argumentation, heretofore undeveloped in China. And with this contribution, Buddhism provided a theoretical basis from which to address concerns about resolving the oppositions and overcoming the errors believed to be rooted in partiality. Owing to the "breadth" of its intuitive base, it provides the means to "erase the distinction between existence and nonexistence and to unite the profane and the religious."[4] Even as we are called on to free ourselves from attachment (caused by the passions) and illusion (of permanence), we must also keep from slipping, at the other extreme as represented by the Hinayanists, into a unilateral vision of aversion for the world and renunciation of life. Refusing to allow that existence might possess any hint of the absolute does not necessarily entail "ridding oneself of all that exists, closing oneself off from hearing and seeing, and remaining forever silent and gloomy."[5] True, because things do not arise of themselves, but depend on external causes and conditions to exist, they do not truly exist; but because they do emerge from these causes and conditions, it is not true that they do not exist. Thus just as "existence is not absolute existence," nonexistence, from a particular point of view, cancels itself out and becomes incapable of constituting "total emptiness." "Insofar as existence is not identical to the absolute, and as nonexistence does not succeed in erasing its own traces, existence and nonexistence differ in name but are, in the end, the same."[6] So the middle way is no more a part of the noumenal world than of the phenomenal world. It is limited to neither side but dissolves their duality and leads to recognition of the identity of extremes — those not just of existence and nonexistence but of religious and profane life, nirvana and samsara, Buddha and other living beings.

Returning now to the subject of blandness: the above extremes constitute the margins of flavor, while its center transcends all their differences. To take up once again the two lines of poetry by Su Dongpo cited earlier: if the "sour" and the "salty" both "are part of what we enjoy," then all we need to do is to situate ourselves at the "center" (relative to those two) and transcend their duality, in order to gain access to true flavor — that which "never fades away."[7]

The two lines preceding this reference to flavor already invoke this ideal of the bland life:

> To experience the world and walk among men,
> To see oneself resting on cloudy peaks.[8]

These two mutually contradictory movements, "leaving the world" and "entering the world," according to one traditional Chinese alternative, are no longer contradictory. Indeed, the reconciliation of the spiritual life and the social life herein implied is all the more compelling to the Chinese literati, ever attuned to the demands of political engagement and hostile to the kind of isolation imposed by monastic existence. The bland, as an existential ideal, makes it possible both to avoid losing oneself in the worldly affairs of the times and to reject the necessity of isolation in a solitary life. Thus the illusory antithesis that had rendered these options mutually exclusive is now nullified within the flavor of the center:

> Terraced pavilions — mountains forests:
> It never was necessary to distinguish between them![9]

The flavor of the center is only attained, then, by those who can keep from being limited to or obsessed by one flavor in particular (whichever it may be), without going so far as to eliminate that flavor. When, rather than favoring one flavor over another, we remain equally open to all of them, we evolve freely through the different flavors and so do away with their incompatibility. Such is the flavor referred to as "limpid" (*qing*): that which, by virtue of its blandness, unifies and reconciles all others. Another poem concludes:

In the world of men, there is flavor:
It is limpidity that one can love.[10]

We can see more clearly now what the center signifies in relation to the margin. But how are we to understand the passage from one to the other? Once again, I believe, the perspective offered by a comparison of cultures can help us. We know that in the Greek tradition the "envelope" (of myth) contains a truth hidden in its core. Whether we look at the margin of flavor or the veil of allegory, an exterior exists that must be penetrated or transcended ("a border" or "clothing") in order to reach the depths. And this doubling of meaning between appearance and reality brings us to true understanding.

Based on this analogy, then, how does this act of overcoming the exterior take place? The virtue of mythopoeia is not so much that of protecting the truth from the eyes of the coarse and common as of stimulating the search for it by obliging us to seek it on another plane. As Proclus (410–485, regarded as the chief representative of the Neoplatonists) tells us in his *Commentarium in Rempublicam Platonis* (Commentary on Plato's *Republic*); (dissertation 6), the more the Homeric myths dramatize ugliness and impurity, the more they inculcate in us a pure idea of the divine. These divinely inspired myths, different from those that are merely didactic, "demonstrate through the preternatural that which, among the gods, surpasses nature; and through the irrational that which is more divine than all reason; and through objects presented to us as ugly that which transcends, by its simplicity, all partial beauty."[11] By presenting an image that is deliberately deformed or monstrous, the figurative aspect of myth does not merely correspond to the "demonic" part of reality — "that which is most deeply rooted in matter" — it obliges us to arrive at a vision diametrically opposed to, and transcendent of, the divine. The more paradoxical and less plausible the image, one might say, the more it forces us to go beyond its literality, to break with perception, to rise to the level of the Intelligible. The trivial leads to the Ideal, and appearance to Truth. We recall the various Silenuses: beneath their grimaces, they concealed an unsuspected treasure. [12] Similarly, the imagistic language of the Holy Scriptures acts as a stimulant, as Clement of Alexandria (known as the Greek Father of the Church, born circa 150) tells us (*Stromatis* 5): the veil of the parable does not merely serve as a screen; it stirs our desire to seek the hidden mystery beneath.[13] Generally speaking, the logic of the symbol is to create as much tension as possible between the literary figure and its object: the exigent appeal of meaning and its implications emanates from this.

And the rest, as we have by now realized, is the transcending to which we are summoned by the bland. Blandness does not demand that we look for another meaning or embark on a quest for a hidden mystery. Rather, it invites us to free ourselves from the differentiating nature of meaning and of all particular and marked flavors. Rather than setting up tension, the blandness of the margin delivers us from all constraining obsessions. It creates *ease*. It unburdens consciousness, for this transcending is not directed and does not lead toward anything other than itself. There is no question, as we have seen, of an Intelligible set in opposition to the perceptible, of a noumenon that is to be preferred to a phenomenon. Nor does the center stand as the hypostasis of anything (not even of Emptiness). True, existence does not exist, but neither is it nonexistent. To be in a position to fully enjoy existence, all one has to do is to resist being subjugated by it. Blandness is precisely this taste of the virtual, the power to evolve and to transform oneself; and, as such, it is inexhaustible. Neither do we find here any Meaning to decode or any Revelation to await. This center is not a Truth set in opposition to falsehood. Instead, all Messages surrender to silence.

In the Buddhist sutra, after each person has taught, in his own way, how to "enter into nonduality" (*advaya*), Vimalakirti simply remains silent, and Manjusri can but approve of this response.[14] At this stage, he who has said nothing provides nothing that can be refuted, and "phonemes, sounds, and ideas have no use." Tasting substitutes for knowing; it is the only true aspiration.

CHAPTER FOURTEEN

Blandness or Strength

Blandness as a value, so long perceived as a paradox, now appears quite obvious: indeed, so obvious, so omnipresent, that it may be difficult to perceive it, let alone utter it. Yet even though it culminates in a sensibility common to all the arts (music, painting, calligraphy, poetry, and the martial arts — not to mention the culinary arts); though it draws its inspiration, in different ways, from all the traditions of Chinese thought (Confucianism, Daoism, and even Buddhism), gaining sustenance from the correlations among them; though it grows out of a value fundamental to all of Chinese civilization (harmony), it is still unlikely that such an understanding of blandness could be universally shared. Besides, had it not ultimately been faced with some contrastive perspective, this notion of blandness would have been in danger of canceling itself out, for harmony pushed to the extreme can only culminate in nothingness. With the complete elimination of difference, all awareness of qualities would disappear. Intelligence, understanding, would lose its grounding and slip into inconsistency. Praise itself would become impossible.

I will not dwell on those things, like the great Song dynasty philosopher Zhu Xi who, in his comments on the poetry of Mei Yaochen, considered such a style not "plain and bland" but

"withered and weak" (the poet being more the target of this criticism than the value he represents).[1] One can always protest that
these people, who were not poets, were lacking in the necessary
sensibility. But this argument loses its currency as soon as we see
that artists, too, rare as they are, are joining in the rebellion
against blandness. The following passage (cited at the beginning
of the preceding chapter) sets up a parallel that already contains
the seeds of future disagreement:

> Liu Zongyuan's poems are inferior to those of Tao Yuanming but
> superior to those of Wei Yingwu. Han Yu's poems excel in their
> *vigor* of *feeling* and *audacity* of expression but are less successful in
> achieving a serene and reserved profundity. The reason why we value
> the dry and bland is that, if the outside is sere, the inside will be lush;
> and apparent blandness contains beauty.[2]

We recall, too, that the first critic to praise poetic blandness,
Sikong Tu, placed his poem "Harmony-Blandness" second in his
series of twenty-four; "Force-Incipiency" was first, since in its
wake blandness was thought to reveal itself. In other words, faced
with the harmonizing power of blandness, there is first a surge of
vitality: when the trace of the brush does not tend toward a fading
away, but presses forward with the violence of an explosion —
when it is still bursting with vehemence and fire, virtually crying
out with passion and life.

It is in this spirit that Han Yu, the Tang poet whose "vigor"
and "audacity" are noted above, denied that blandness could serve
as inspiration. In his view, inspiration must be sought in surges of
vitality and intense psychological concentration. He who devotes
himself exclusively to his art has little to fear from worldly dis-
tractions. It is thus pointless to try to detach oneself from the
world, as advocated by Buddhists. This poet, known primarily as

one of the most important advocates for a return to the Confucian tradition of the ancients, was in principle no more opposed to emotions than he was doubtful of the reality of external phenomena (which were thought to correspond to those emotions). These phenomena, according to Confucian thought, grow out of the great process of nature — the regular ebb and flow between the visible and the Invisible. And this capacity for constancy in the production of the beings and things of this world forms, through its influence, the basis for morality. As for art, it is the spontaneous response of inner emotion stirred by the transformations taking place in the external world. Man's fecundity is the product of this impulsive force, which links him to the universe.

And once again the art of calligraphy serves as the favored ground for demonstration. If, this author tells us, the script of as great a master of the Tang as Zhang Xu is so remarkable, it is because it occupied him utterly and because he projected therein his deepest and most varied feelings: "his joy or his anger, his anguish, torments, happiness, resentment, longing — his drunkenness, too — along with his boredom and even his rebellion."[3] By the same token, far from cutting himself off from the spectacle of the world, he expressed it in all its intensity and violent contrasts: the tranquillity of nature and the wildness of warfare, all living species, mountains and flowers, insects and stars. His writing contained "the wind and the rain," "water and fire," "thunder, lightning, song and dance," and transformed itself unceasingly in its encounter with life's infinite dynamism. The profusion of things, the power of phenomena, all that thrills or provokes tears — the great calligrapher breathed them into his brush strokes, so much so that "one loses sight of their end" and his work overflows with vitality.

The path that leads to this art, then, is that of passion — of *attachment*. The conditions for embarking on this road are "possessing a clear awareness of what conforms to our interest and what harms it" and "allowing nothing to escape our attention": "that an emotion burns within, and the desire inspired by this interest is ready to confront anything in order to move forward; and, whether we win or lose, we feel ourselves to be carried away and completely engaged."[4] In this way, when this emotional engagement, taken to the extreme, discharges itself in writing, "the ideal is not far." Such is the tension that electrifies the Master's calligraphy and lends it its powerful fascination. Born of intoxication and pathos, it incites us to exultation.

In contrast, there is someone else (Gao Xian, to whom this letter is written) who, good Buddhist that he is, "holds life and death to be equal" and "freed himself from all exterior attachments": "His mind is so serene that no longer does anything arise within; and the world, in his eyes, is so bland that it no longer has the power to ignite any desires." "Blandness and detachment" have thus destroyed his personality and plunged it into lethargy. The individual is "extinguished" and "atonal," and his writing, fatally, "no longer resembles anything at all."[5]

But does detachment really extinguish personality, and does blandness render us numb? We see how this conflict in values becomes ideological and moral as well as aesthetic. And this debate takes on even greater importance during the Song, when literati (happy to be called "lay brothers") and Buddhist monks (who composed poetry) carried on the process of osmosis, which had begun centuries earlier, between Buddhism and the Chinese tradition. Two centuries later, Su Dongpo, the author of the subtle distinction between the margin and the center mentioned earlier, would thus defend blandness in connection with emotion. This response is addressed to a monk, a friend of the poet's and a lover of poetry:

You have studied suffering and emptiness,
The myriad thoughts, in you, are as cold ashes.[6]

Obligatory preface: from his spiritual heights, the monk has been able to recognize the roots of suffering, expose the emptiness of phenomena, and so his heart has become immune to disturbances. How, in this condition, is he to take on the work of poetry? It is here, then, that he mentions the criticism concerning blandness in calligraphy we read earlier: "deadened" as one is when devoted to "blandness-detachment," is it still possible to manifest any "vigor and élan"? The poet then speaks in his own voice:

Looking at things more closely, it is not like this. . . .
If you want to perfect your poetic expression,
Do not reject encounters with calm and emptiness:
For calm brings the various movements to completion;
And emptiness embraces all possible worlds.[7]

Here the basic argument is presented: the calm inner world and the intuition of emptiness do not cut us off from emotion. To the contrary, because emotion no longer disturbs us, we apprehend it all the more clearly and are thus able to enjoy it. Fits of passion and its exuberance are charged with making our subjectivity superficial and reducing our sensitivity. When we attain the world of blandness, feelings distract us no longer, and emotive experience is purified, clarified. The mind, in keeping with the old metaphor of still water or mirrors, reflects all the better the infinite wealth of the life within: not just one particular feeling, lived within the confines of its limitations and contingencies, but all feeling as it becomes whole and inclusive, returned to its virtual state.

This discussion may also be applied analogously to painting. From a strictly technical standpoint, as we saw at the beginning, blandness was first associated with paleness: color is less vivid, and ink — diluted — is more limpid, as opposed to the brightness of colors (the five colors, analogous to the five sounds and the five flavors). It is characteristic of Chinese painting to play with the opposition of light and dark (*dannong*), as with all the other contrastive pairs that lend dynamism to representation (empty and full, dense and sparse...). But paleness can also characterize the overall tone of a painting, or its atmosphere, and this is when "plain and bland" becomes a style in itself, analogous to poetic blandness. We can trace this tradition back as early as the tenth century when it was represented by Dong Yuan and Juran. Then the preferred landscape was found around the lower reaches of the Blue River, the area known as "South of the River," or "Jiangnan": vast stretches of water open into space, hills undulate in the distance like yet other waves. No jutting angles or rocky precipices appear among these hills that dissolve into the mist like "scattered flax." A hazy atmosphere softens and blurs the contours of the land.

As it was in the case of the poet's inward journey, so it is for that of the painter; only with age does he (such as Juran, Dong Yuan's disciple) arrive at the "plain and bland." The mists that arise in his landscapes are, we are simply told, "limpid and unctuous" (*qingrun*).[8] The following commentary on the master's work, however, is somewhat less succinct:

> Dong Yuan knows how to be plain and bland, natural and authentic [*pingdan tianzhen*], to the utmost degree. No one under the Tang could compare... [figure 14.1].
>
> [In his landscapes] mountain peaks appeared and disappeared; clouds and fog were illuminated or darkened. He drew upon no artifice but was spontaneously spurred to natural and true expression.

Figure 14.1. Blandness and vitality. Landscape attributed to Dong Yuan,
10th century (National Museum of Taipei).

The mist's color is of a deep blue; trunks and branches rise up, vigorous and straight. Everything here breathes life.[9]

Like blandness in poetry, blandness in painting bathes the landscape in absence: the various forms appear only to be withdrawn, opening upon distances that transcend them. But this blandness does not lead to insubstantiality; the trees exude an inner intensity. The basis for the bland is, once again, the natural.

The praise of pictorial blandness invokes the same arguments; its simplicity reminds us of that of the ancients who were opposed to the aesthetic of brightness and seduction, of the sensational and facile, to which so many of their contemporaries had succumbed.[10] The connotations of blandness are still the same as well: "calm," "vagueness," "solitude," and the feeling of "unfetteredness."[11] The dialectic of inversion that had valorized poetic blandness reappears here unchanged: what is simple is "all the more complete," what is bland is "all the more dense and concentrated."[12] Blandness is more intense than any outright manifestation of intensity. Just as "easy, unaffected openness" gives rise to efficacy, and "calm" opens the way to perfect understanding, or "remoteness" extends the reach of meaning, blandness enables one most readily to achieve originality.[13] As far as their implications have been extended, "plenitude," "blandness," and the "absence of intentionality" are no less endowed with that "impossibility of incompleteness" (in terms of both meaning and representation) — something, says one critic, much more exigent than any completed painting. A return to the logic of Buddhist formulation: the "common" does not stand opposite to the "extraordinary" (or the "particular"), but encompasses it.[14]

In painting as elsewhere, blandness requires a transformation, a process begun as early as during the painter's training. Indeed, this is what defines it. "When we imitate the ancients, we worry right from the start that [our work] 'does not resemble theirs'; then we worry that it 'resembles theirs too closely.' If it doesn't resemble theirs, it is because we have not gone far enough in studying their technique; and if it resembles theirs too closely, then it is no longer our own technique." The conclusion: only when both technique and originality are equally "forgotten," when their mutual opposition is transcended, can the "bland and natural" (*pingdan tianran*) emerge. [15] More generally, change and transformation are essential to art. The unique and extraordinary can only be achieved through the common and plain, and blandness of expression presumes originality. [16]

Furthermore, from the viewpoint of the art enthusiast, the ability to appreciate a painting also depends on a process of transformation (in which one may or may not engage: which is why the most beautiful painting — the one that demands the most of the viewer — is ever at risk of not being appreciated [17]). "At first glance, it is plain and bland," but "the longer one looks at it, the more apparent its spiritual dimension [*chu guan pingdan, jiu shi shen ming*]." In contrast, "what first appears beautiful loses its fascination as soon as one looks away from it." [18] The richness of the bland lies in its capacity to offer us an opportunity to transform our gaze into consciousness and to go endlessly deeper. Rather than providing immediate gratification of our most superficial tastes, a bland painting beckons our inner being to immerse itself in it ever further. And so painting and consciousness evolve together in harmony.

There is general agreement in China concerning these values. But I do not want to conclude without offering a glimpse at an aesthetic that takes an opposing stance and succeeds in establishing painterly values on the basis of strength and intensity. We recall the paintings with which we began this essay: pale paintings, composed of the rare brush stroke, opening onto vast, empty spaces (of sky and of water), where nothing forces itself on the gaze and everything is equal and seems on the verge of disappearing. Although first inspired by the same tradition (that of Dong Yuan and Juran), Wang Meng, a contemporary of this painter (Ni Zan), developed the art of landscape painting in exactly the opposite direction. The objects cluster and crowd together rather than dispersing across the plane; they encumber the space rather than allowing it to breathe; they twist back on themselves, or push violently against one another, rather than emerging in calm and solitude. The density of the line, the brightness of the colors, the intricacy of detail reinforce the impression of luxuriance and profusion. The contrast of shadow and light (with the light emanating from a mystifying source), as well as the fragile balance of the composition (thrusting dizzyingly upward), dangerously draws attention to the tension. A proliferation of matter and form converges on us from all directions: the entire universe seems to be sucking itself into a great metamorphic propulsion, pushing itself against the threshold of chaos.

Of the many vistas of the Great Lake (Tai Hu), one painter has rendered its broadly spaced meadows, level perspective, and rarefied and sparse vegetation (figure 14.2). Another singles out the caves carved out by the water at the base of its islets (figure 14.3). There is nothing here to articulate or illuminate the movement of things; the topography reveals itself convulsively before our eyes like some mountainous mass in the process of solidifying. Matter is at work everywhere: twists and folds push at each other; everything pierces through and retracts. The space is saturated; the turmoil of the scene has reached an extreme. Even the lake, the natural place for experiencing repose and the erasure of form, just barely appears in an upper corner of the scroll (while a river, gushing out of the cave, occupies the foreground). Nor are the waters

Figure 14.2. Landscape of blandness III. Landscape painting
by Ni Zan (National Museum of Taipei).

Figure 14.3. Landscape of density. Landscape painting by Wang Meng,
14th century (National Museum of Taipei).

allowed to flow freely; they are agitated by the ambient distur-
bance. One is tempted to say that they are contained by the flim-
siest of nets. Amid their tortuous twists, a few solid masses just
manage to insert their rectilinear forms, like so many isolated cells
in a tumultuous world. And each is inhabited by a solitary and
seemingly indifferent figure.

A landscape like this does not beckon toward the spiritual
deepening we found to be *de rigueur* in literati painting. But this
does not mean that we can easily turn away from it, any more than
we can from a landscape of which the intensity — precisely because
it is manifest — quickly exhausts itself. This expressionism arrests
our gaze and fascinates us. The longer we contemplate this landscape, the more it oppresses us. At the furthest extreme from the
bland landscape purified of the opacity of things, this landscape
extracts from their sheer excessiveness and turbulence a powerful
effect. Presence rather than withdrawal completely occupies our
attention. The landscape opens not upon the freeing from consciousness but upon a kind of fantastic recklessness. (Ni Zan, this
painter's friend, was able to praise this bursting forth of vigor and
power: "It could even raise up a bronze tripod!")

This world in upheaval is indeed one that was lived in by both
painters: the end of the Mongolian occupation; the crisis and dis-
order that accompanied the establishment of the new reign. But
one of them sought to distance himself from it: he gave up his
estates, freed himself from his attachments, in order to move
more serenely through this troubled epoch. The other pursued an
official career and remained involved in politics. Accused of being
closely connected to a minister who fell out of favor, he eventually died in prison. But by then his tortured painting had already
recounted for us, with a dramatic flourish, the anguish of living.

CHAPTER FIFTEEN

Transcendence Is Natural

Does all this suggest that there is a Chinese "Romanticism" in search of the intense, passionate effect, standing in opposition to the deliberate constraint and "trimming back" of maturity? If so, then the discreetness associated with the bland would recall the virtues of classicism. In a selection of "writings" — the famous understatement — we find this lesson: the great artist, says André Gide, "strives for banality." "The greatest work of art is the one that will at first be overlooked, the one nobody will even notice." Such a work is the expression of an equilibrium in which "the most contradictory qualities...breathe" in unison. Just as with the bland work of art, it is necessary to "contemplate [classic works] over a long period," "for them to surrender their deepest significance," "so secret is their inner vibration." Then, behind their "apparent aloofness," one may discover "their most exquisite quality": their "reserve."[1]

But the comparison ends here, not wrong so much as unreliable, losing its validity if taken past a certain point. We may well perceive, here and there, some accord between bursts of passion (which can be the result of new forces or emotions that are impossible to contain) and emphatic expression (thus linking psychology, mores, and style); but the meaning of blandness overruns this framework — or, more precisely, simply passes through it. It does not limit itself to the lesson of the value of discreetness, but is rooted in a metaphysical notion: that of *neutrality*. (I employ the term "metaphysical" here only for its usefulness in connection with Western traditions, and with the same reservations as before, because, as we have seen, blandness evades metaphysics, immediately dissolving any construct that it might set forth.) Manifesting itself as a kind of style, blandness nevertheless calls for a transformation of existence; the same word, as we have seen, speaks of both the insipidity of things and the detachment of self. In order to convey its comprehensive reach, traditional Chinese writers resort to a Buddhist term and speak of "world," or *jing*.

Blandness is experienced by the whole consciousness and expresses our *being in the world* at its most radical. We can take the measure of the bland with even greater precision if we abandon the traditional opposition between classicism and Romanticism and look to what followed (as expressed in the sensibilities of French art at the end of the nineteenth century), when poetry began to break through into the world and the spirit to become the preferred terrain for all manner of inquiry — after the epoch of the grand lyrical rapture, when the impetuous urge for excitement began to ebb and the value of an inner openness to the world began to emerge:

> Close your eyes halfway,
> Fold your arms across your breast,
> And from your sleeping heart
> Banish all plans, forever.[2]

"Repose, silence, relaxation, opening," comments Jean-Pierre Richard in his fine article "Fadeur de Verlaine" (The blandness of Verlaine), a phrase that could just as well describe this traditional

Chinese aesthetic value.[3] In such qualities as his "quietism of the senses," in his apprehension of the world at a moment of presence-absence which renders that world less determined, in the temptation of aloofness and indifference (that, in the end, characterizes many aspects of his development), the "Verlainian being" is, in effect, seduced by the blandness of an "existence ready for extinction": odors are "evanescent," landscapes "submerged in unreality by the rise of mists and twilights," and sounds "already imbued with silence."[4]

But this penchant of sensibility cannot, in Verlaine's work, lead to any foundational realization — a fact that modifies, in turn, the sensation of blandness itself. Verlainian blandness, a matter of a *softening* or *wilting*, uncovers the charms of a slow swoon (where one's half-dead sensations are being cut off from their source) much more than the allure of plenitude (that of a totality not yet divided). It acquires its depth and richness from what was but is no longer — not from what it is in virtuality (before dissipating itself in actualization). Because Verlainian blandness cannot anchor itself in any fundamental neutrality of world and experience (which in China would be that of the center or the Dao), because its desire for non-differentiation does not lead to any "common ground of sensibility," and because it therefore remains a purely subjective quest, separated from the vitality of the things of the world, it cannot endure as such. As Richard shows, the taste of the bland is thenceforth driven to become, by itself, ever more complex. Thus when the art of dissonance (so prized by Verlaine) reawakens his awareness of the threat of atrophy, a certain *acuteness* challenges the indecisiveness of the gray-toned melody and tears it apart: the "moment" is "both very *vague* and very *sharp*."

And so a far cry from the infinite polyvalence of Chinese blandness (which leads to harmony), the flavor of neutrality appears in the writings of the *poète maudit* (the "accursed poet") as a kind of hesitancy or irresolution that, by virtue of its desired effect of ambivalence, has the power to seduce our consciousness—but also to disturb it. The bland taste becomes one that is *bittersweet*, from which the poet draws an artificial pleasure (in the sense of Charles Baudelaire's "artificial paradises"). A "doubtful," somewhat suspicious equilibrium: blandness in this case becomes an "irritating" provocation.[5] This gray flavor obtains from something *deliberate*, as in the following verse: "Irritated this *deliberately* insipid heart."

The same may be observed in the field of music; Gabriel Fauré, for example, echoes Verlaine in this regard. What they share is the notion of "mutedness." Vladimir Jankélévitch shows at length how the "spirit of understatement" and "evasive language" inspired the composer's *La Bonne Chanson* and "Fêtes galantes": the characters "seem to us so deliciously dreamy"; they "lightly skim across the surface of emotions without accentuating them"; "neutral, subdued, and inconsistent."[6] "Seeking out the half-light; painting in halftones, speaking in intimations and hushed tones": this is the ideal. Soft-pedaling the piano "muffles and distills," and a gentle touch of the keys, too, is the art of "light brushing across the surface."[7] But Jankélévitch also warns us that this "inexpressive expressiveness" is a ploy, and this indifference is affected.[8] If aversion to the loud pedal, the "distrust of the *rallentando* and the *rubato*"—so apparent in the piano work of Fauré—reflects a rejection of great Romantic flourishes (an attitude shared by his whole generation), it is still true that this *plain style* that "levels and makes uniform" is undermined by tactical strategies and goals of its own.[9] Beneath its anodyne facade we find a "slyly seditious language": a "pseudo conformism" that hides "a diffuse transgression."[10] This aloofness is a mask, and this blandness a false naïveté.

In Verlaine, the bland is a wilting flower that refuses to die, infinitely seductive in its air of pseudo existence (which envelops us as well). Through blandness, the very notion of reality ends up lost. In order to reestablish his connection with being, in order to escape the disturbing enigma of the non-differentiation of things into which he feels his consciousness dissolving, Verlaine reacts by abruptly renouncing the temptation of blandness, of languor, and embracing transcendence in its place. He thus passes from the "that" of perceptual indeterminateness to the "He" of Revelation.[11] From this point on, he suspends before his eyes the Truth (of Christ), takes on the most beatific of Epinal images (in *Sagesse*), and meticulously reconstructs all the "compartments" of his spirit (on the basis of which he can clearly organize all reality).[12] And then from this newly acquired Faith emanates a "pure, unfiltered light":

> Outlined with a black stroke
> All things revealed
> Displaying to you duty
> In its rough, unpolished form.[13]

This is the price for returning things to a state of clarity and definition. Verlaine is done with blandness: contrast erases neutrality and reestablishes certainty.

But the insipidity of traditional China, as represented by the limpidity of water (the basis for all flavors), is neither mere understatement nor affected (or complicated) blandness. Rather, it constitutes a transformation — a conversion — the "beyond" of which is already contained within, leading consciousness to the *root* of the real, to the *center* from which the process of things flows. It is the way of deepening (toward the simple, the natural, the essential), of detachment (from the particular, the individual, the contingent). This transcendence does not open onto another world, but is lived as immanence itself; viewed from this perspective, the two terms finally cease being opposites. Blandness is this experience of transcendence reconciled with nature — and divested of faith.

Notes

TRANSLATOR'S PREFACE

1. Tzvetan Todorov, "Letter from Paris," *Salmagundi: A Quarterly of the Humanities and Social Sciences* 109–10 (Winter/Spring 1996), pp. 3–15.

2. "A Philosophical Use of China: An Interview with François Jullien," *Thesis Eleven* 57 (May 1999), pp. 113–30. This is an edited translation of an interview originally published in *Le Débat* 91 (1996), pp. 164–92.

3. *The Propensity of Things: Toward a History of Efficacy in China*, trans. Janet Lloyd (New York: Zone Books, 1995), p. 13.

4. See Zhang Longxi's reaction to the 1996 interview published in *Le Débat*, cited above, in his "Hanxue yu Zhong Xi wenhua de duili – du Yulian xiansheng fangtanlu you gan" (Sinology and the opposition of Chinese and Western Cultures: A response to reading an interview with Mr. Jullien), *Ershiyi shiji* 53 (June 1999), pp. 144–48. For an extended exposition of Zhang's call for circumspection in the comparative study of China, see his *Mighty Opposites: From Dichotomies to Differences in the Comparative Study of China* (Stanford, CA: Stanford University Press, 1998).

5. François Jullien and Thierry Marchaisse, *Penser d'un dehors (La Chine)* (Paris: Seuil, 2000), p. 53.

6. Cited in *ibid.*, p. 53, from Roland Barthes, *Oeuvres complètes, 1966-1973* (Paris: Seuil, 1994), vol. 2, p. 748.

7. A point aptly made by Haun Saussy in his review of *The Propensity of Things* in *Journal of Asian Studies* 55, no. 4 (Nov. 1996), pp. 984–87.

8. Jullien and Marchaisse, *Penser d'un dehors*, p. 247.

9. Jun'ichiro Tanizaki, *In Praise of Shadows*, trans. Thomas J. Harper and Edward G. Seidensticker (New Haven, CT: Leete's Island Books, 1977).

10. For the scholarly work referred to, see, for example, Jonathan Chaves, *Mei Yao-ch'en and the Development of Early Sung Poetry* (New York: Columbia University Press, 1976); Peter Charles Sturman, *Mi Fu: Style and the Art of Calligraphy in Northern Song China* (New Haven, CT: Yale University Press, 1997).

PROLOGUE

1. François Jullien, *Procès ou creation: Une Introduction à la pensée des lettrés chinois* (Paris: Seuil, 1989).

CHAPTER ONE: A CHANGE OF SIGN

1. Roland Barthes, *Alors la Chine?* (Paris: Christian Bourgois, 1975), p. 14.

2. Roland Barthes, *L'Empire des signes* (Paris: Flammarion, 1970). See also the English translation by Richard Howard, *Empire of Signs* (New York: Hill and Wang, 1982).

3. Barthes, *Alors la Chine?* p. 13.

4. *Ibid.*, p. 10.

5. *Ibid.*, p. 12.

6. *Ibid.*, p. 12. Pilin-pikong is the transliteration of the Chinese expression, "criticize (*pi*) Lin [Biao] and criticize Confucius (Kong)," current in 1974 when Roland Barthes and the other members of Tel quel traveled to China. Lin Biao had been named second in command of the Chinese Communist Party in 1966, at the beginning of the Cultural Revolution, making him Mao Zedong's heir apparent until he mysteriously died in a plane crash in 1971. This sloganistic linking of a contemporary political target with a "reactionary" figure of ancient times — especially Confucius — was a typical feature of the ideological movements that arose at the end of the Cultural Revolution — TRANS.

7. I have translated these quotations from the French. See G.W.F. Hegel, *Leçons sur l'histoire de la philosophie*, trans. J. Gibelin (Paris: Gallimard, 1954), p. 241. For an alternative translation in English, see G.W.F. Hegel, *Lectures on the*

History of Philosophy, 3 vols., trans. E.S. Haldane and Frances H. Simson (London: Kegan Paul, Trench, Trübner and Company, 1892–1896), vol. 1, pp. 120–21. —TRANS.

8. "Shu er," in *Lunyu*, 7.10. All references to Chinese texts are from the *Siku quanshu* edition unless otherwise noted.

9. *Ibid.*, 7.10n.

10. *Ibid.*, 7.10n.

11. *Ibid.*, 7.22.

12. *Ibid.*, 7.22n.

13. *Ibid.*, 7.22n.

CHAPTER THREE: BLANDNESS-DETACHMENT

1. *Laozi*, ß35, in *Laozi Daodejing*, ann. Wang Bi, in *Zhuzi jicheng*, vol. 3, p. 20.

2. *Laozi*, ß63, vol. 3, p. 38.

3. "Inner Chapter 7: Yingdiwang," in *Zhuangzi jishi*, in *Zhuzi jicheng*, vol. 3, p. 132.

4. Matthew 5:13; see also Luke 14:34–35 and Mark 9:50.

CHAPTER FOUR: THE SENSE OF NEUTRALITY

1. *Gantong*, first used in the "Appended Commentaries" of the *Book of Change*, refers to the notion that all change occurs through an unending chain of stimulus and response. —TRANS.

2. *Zhongyong*, ß1.

3. I have chosen the term "Mean" rather than "Center" here because it has been the conventional translation of *zhong* when it is used to refer specifically to this Confucian virtue. —TRANS.

4. *Zhongyong*, ß11.

5. *Ibid.*, ß33.

6. *Ibid.*, ß15.

CHAPTER FIVE: BLANDNESS IN SOCIETY

1. "Outer Chapter 20: Shanmu," in *Zhuangzi jishi*, in *Zhuzi jicheng*, vol. 3, p. 300.

2. *Ibid.*, p. 299.

3. *Ibid.*, p. 300.

4. *Ibid.*, p. 300.

5. "Biaoji," in *Liji*, in *Liji zhengyi*, 3 vols., ed. Li Xuele, (Beijing: Beijing University Press, 1999), vol. 3, p. 1493.

CHAPTER SIX: OF CHARACTER: THE BLAND AND THE PLAIN

1. *Zhongyong*, ß1.

2. Liu Shao (third century), "Jiu zheng," in *Renwuzhi* (The treatise on human abilities), I.1b. This treatise is the first and most important Chinese work devoted to the study of personality; see J.K. Shryock's introduction to Liu Shao, *The Study of Human Abilities*, trans. and ed. J.K. Shryock (New Haven, CT: American Oriental Society, 1937), p. 96.

3. *Ibid.*, Liu Bing's commentary.

4. "Gongsun Chou," part 1, ß2, and "Wan zhang," part 2, ß1, in *Mencius*.

5. "Jiuzheng," in *Renwuzhi*, 1.1b.

6. *Ibid.*, 1.4a.

7. Osvald Sirén, *La Sculpture chinoise, du Ve au XIVe siècles* (Paris: Annales du Musée Guimet, 1925), pp. 33 and 36–37.

CHAPTER SEVEN: "LINGERING TONE" AND "LINGERING TASTE"

1. "Benwei," in *Lüshi chunqiu*, in *Zhuzi jicheng*, vol. 6, p. 141.

2. "Miuchengxun," in *Huainanzi*, in *Zhuzi jicheng*, vol. 7, p. 158.

3. Yueji," in *Liji*, "in *Liji Zhengyi*, 3 vols., ed. Li Xuele (Beijing: Beijing University Press, 1999), vol. 2, p. 1081. For a detailed description of the physical attributes of and techniques for playing the *qin*, or zither, see Kenneth J. DeWoskin, *A Song for One or Two: Music and the Concept of Art in Early China* (Ann Arbor: University of Michigan, Center for Chinese Studies, 1982), pp. 120–24. — TRANS.

4. Kong Yingda's commentary to the above passage, in "Yueji," p. 1081.

CHAPTER EIGHT: SILENT MUSIC

1. As in *Lunyu*, 15.11 and 17.18.

2. "Outer Chapter 13: Tiandao," in *Zhuangzi jishi*, in *Zhuzi jicheng*, vol. 3, p. 209.

3. *Laozi*, ß12 in *Laozi Daodejing*, ann. Wang Bi, in *Zhuangzi jishi*, vol. 3, p. 6.

4. "Outer Chapter 12: Tiandi," in *Zhuangzi jishi*, in *Zhuzi jicheng*, vol. 3, p. 185.

5. In the *Laozi*, for example, we find the passage: "Being and nonbeing give rise to each other; the difficult and the easy bring about each other; the long and the short signify in comparison with each other; the high and the low determine each other; tone and sound harmonize with each other." *Laozi*, ß2, pp. 1–2.

6. *Laozi*, ß41, p. 26.

7. Wang Bi's commentary on the above-quoted line of *ibid.*, p. 26.

8. Wang Bi's commentary on *ibid.*, p. 7.

9. "Inner Chapter 2: Qiwulun," in *Zhuangzi jishi*, in *Zhuzi jicheng*, vol. 3, p. 36.

10. *Ibid.*, p. 36.

11. *Ibid.*, p. 36.

12. "Xianjin," in *Lunyu* , 11.26.

13. Su Dongpo, "Songs in Honor of the Eighteen Arhats," no. 16, in *Dongpo quanji* , 98.14a–b.

14. Wang Shizhen, "Qing yan lei," in *Daijingtang shihua*, 3 vols. (Beijing: Renmin wenxue chubanshe, 1982), vol. 3, p. 88.

15. *Songshu*, 93.16b; see also A.R. Davis, *Tao Yüan-ming: His Works and Their Meaning* (New York: Cambridge University Press, 1983), vol. 2, p. 168.

16. That is, from the material strings themselves. — TRANS.

CHAPTER NINE: THE BLANDNESS OF SOUND

1. Ruan Ji, "Yuelun," in *Xinyi Ruan Ji shiwenji*, ed. Lin Jiali (Taipei: Sanmin shuju, 2001), p. 86.

2. Li Bo, "Sent to Prefect Yuan of Jiao, Recalling a Past Outing," in *Quan Tangshi*, 172.1770.

3. "Tangwen," in *Liezi*, 5.15b–16a.

4. Li Bo, "In Jinling, Listening to Censor Han Play the Flute," in *Quan Tangshi*, 184.1877.

5. Li Bo, "Upon Hearing Monk Jun of Sichuan Playing the Zither," in *Quan Tangshi*, 183.1868.

6. This is Guo Pu's elucidation of a line in the *Shan hai jing* (Classic of mountains and seas) which says that on Feng Mountain there are nine bells that ring in response to the frost. In the "Zhong Shan jing" chapter of *Shan hai jing jiaozhu*, ed. Yuan Ke (Shanghai: Shanghai guji, 1980), p. 165.

7. Parallelism is the practice, common in Chinese classical writings, of juxtaposing two lines or phrases in such a way as to stir the reader's awareness of analogous, contrastive, or even transformative relationships between corresponding words in the paired lines. — TRANS.

8. Bo Juyi, "[Playing the] Five-String [Zither] ," in *Quan Tangshi*, 426.4697.

9. Bo Juyi, "A Zither at Night," in *Quan Tangshi*, 430.4752.

10. Bo Juyi, "While Playing the Zither on a Boat at Night," in *Quan Tangshi*, 447.5019.

11. Bo Juyi, "On a Clear Night, I Feel the Urge to Play the Zither," in *Quan Tangshi*, 428.4721. For more complete references and a good analysis of the question, see the unpublished thesis of Florence Hu-Sterk, "Esthétique musicale et la poésie des Tang" (Université de Paris VIII, 1991).

CHAPTER TEN: BLANDNESS'S CHANGE OF SIGNS IN LITERATURE

1. Wang Chong, "Ziji," in *Lunheng*, 30.8b–9a.

2. Lu Ji, "Wen fu," in *Wenfu Shipin yizhu*, ed. and ann. Yang Ming (Shanghai: Shanghai guji, 1999), p. 19.

3. "Pure talk" (*qingtan*) refers to the practice of discussing philosophical matters, very much the mode among literati during this period. For anecdotes celebrating the talents and personalities of the ablest practitioners of "pure talk," see Liu Yiqing, *A New Account of Tales of the World*, trans. and ann. Richard B. Mather (Minneapolis: University of Minnesota Press, 1976). — TRANS.

4. Zhong Hong, preface to *Shipin*, 1.2a.

5. Zhong Hong, *Shipin*, 2.4a.

6. This is apparent in two important works of literary criticism: [Liu Xie's] *Wenxin diaolong* and [Zhong Hong's] *Shipin* [see Appendix A]. [Indeed, it is of particular interest that the *Shipin* contains remarks of both types: those taking blandness as a negative quality (as in the quotations cited here), and those considering it a positive attribute, as we find referenced in n. 10 below. — TRANS.]

7. Liu Xie, "Qingcai," in *Wenxin diaolong*. [See especially the "coda" to this chapter: "Dense coloration that lacks feeling / Will always cloy when we savor (*wei*) it." In Liu Xie, *Wenxin diaolong zhu*, ed. and ann. Fan Wenlan (Taipei: Xuehai, 1988), p. 539. Translated here by Stephen Owen, from his *Readings in Chinese Literary Thought* (Cambridge, MA: Harvard University Press, 1992), p. 245. — TRANS.]

8. See, for example, Liu Xie, "Wuse," in *Wenxin diaolong*, pp. 693–94. [In this description of the function of *xing*, Jullien uses the expression "symbolization" rather loosely. In a particularly relevant passage of this chapter of the *Wenxin diaolong*, Liu Xie presents a series of examples of *xing* from the *Shijing* — *The Book of Odes* — in which images from nature are juxtaposed with scenes from human experience. These suggestive and open-ended juxtapositions invite analogical interpretations and, as a literary practice, have long been understood as expressive of man's intimate relation with nature and the spontaneity of the singers' response to the world around them. For an in-depth discussion of *xing* (translated in English as "incitation") as compared with the Western practice of metaphor and symbol, see Pauline Yu, *The Reading of Imagery in the Chinese Tradition* (Princeton, NJ: Princeton University Press, 1987). — TRANS.]

9. Liu Xie, "Yinxiu," in *Wenxin diaolong*, p. 633.

10. Zhong Hong, *Shipin*, 1.3a.

11. Jiaoran, *Shishi*. See Jiaoran, *Wujuanben Jiaoran Shi Shi* (Taipei: Guangwen shuju, 1982), pp. 7–8.

12. Sima Xiangru (179–118 B.C.E.) is celebrated as the greatest writer of *fu*, or "rhyme-prose," in the history of Chinese poetry. Jullien is referring here to the famous story recounting how Sima, penniless after having failed to find employment at court, returns to Sichuan, where he falls in love with the young widow Zhuo Wenjun. He gains her favor with his musical and poetic talents but

fails to win over her father. When the father refuses the couple financial support after they marry, they open a wineshop together. — TRANS.

13. Sikong Tu, "Chongdan," in *Ershi si shipin* (Twenty-four poetic modes), in *Shipin jijie*, ed. Guo Shaoyu (Beijing: Renmin wenxue, 1981), pp. 5–7.

14. Sikong Tu, "Qili," in *Shipin jijie*, p. 18.

15. Sikong Tu, "Qingqi," in *Shipin jijie*, p. 30.

16. Sikong Tu, "Dianya," in *Shipin jijie*, p. 12.

CHAPTER ELEVEN: THE IDEOLOGY OF BLANDNESS

1. Mei Yaochen, "While Reading the Poetry of Scholar Shao, Du Tingzhi Suddenly Arrived... ," in *Wanlingji*, 46.9b.

2. Mei Yaochen, "Preface to the *Collected Poems of Mr. Lin Hejing*," in *Wanlingji*, 60.1b. [Jullien's translation of *mei* as "plenitude" is based on Mencius, "Jin xin," 7b.25, "Plenitude (of goodness) is beauty." — TRANS.]

3. As in Wei Qingzhi, *Shiren yuxie* 10.11a–29b.

4. Wu Ke, *Canghai shihua*, in *Lidai shihua xubian*, 2 vols., ed. Ding Fubao (Beijing: Zhonghua shuju, 1983), vol. 1, p. 328.

5. Wei Qingzhi, "Pingdan," in *Shiren yuxie*, 10.11a and 10.15a.

6. Wu Ke, *Canghai shihua*, p. 331.

7. Ouyang Xiu, "Offered to Mr. Shi, upon Reading the Writings of Messrs. Zhang and Li," *Wenzhongji* 2.3b.

8. André Gide, *Journal, 1939–1942* (Paris: Gallimard, 1946), p. 82.

9. Ouyang Xiu, "Harmonizing Again with [Mei] Shengshu's Response," in *Wenzhongji*, 5.6a.

10. Ouyang Xiu, "Night Outing at Shuigu, Sent to Mei Shengshu," in *Wenzhongji*, 2.6b.

11. Mei Yaochen, "Harmonizing with the Rhymes of Master Yan," in *Wanlingji*, 28.11b–12a.

12. Mei Yaochen, "答中道小疾見寄 ," in *Wanlingji*, 24.16a–b.

13. Ouyang Xiu, "Funerary Inscription for Mei Shengshu [that is, Mei Yaochen]," *Wenzhongji*, 33.9b.

14. Mei Yaochen, "Preface to the *Collected Poems of Mr. Lin Hejing*."

CHAPTER TWELVE: FLAVOR-BEYOND-THE-FLAVORFUL, LANDSCAPE-
BEYOND-LANDSCAPES

1. See François Jullien, *La Valeur allusive* (Paris: Ecole Française d'Extrême-Orient, 1985), p. 152.

2. Sikong Tu, "Letter on Poetry to Mr. Li," in *Shipin jijie*, ed. Guo Shaoyu (Beijing: Renmin wenxue, 1981), p. 47.

3. *Ibid.*, p. 47.

4. *Ibid.*, p. 47.

5. Sikong Tu, "Letter on Poetic Criticism to Mr. Wang Jia," in *Shipin jijie*, p. 50.

6. Sikong Tu, "Letter on poetry to Mr. Li," p. 48.

7. Wang Wei, "Luchai," (Deer enclosure), in *Wang Youcheng ji jianzhu*, ed. and ann. Zhao Diancheng (Shanghai: Shanghai guji, 1998), p. 243.

8. Li Dongyang, *Litang shihua*, as cited in *Tangshi sanbaishou jishi* (Taipei: Yiwen yinshuguan, 1977), p. 410.

9. Liu Dacheng, ed., *Tangshi sanbaishou xinshang* (Taipei: Wenhua tushuguan, 1984), p. 271.

10. Tao Yuanming, "Drinking Wine #5," in *Tao Yuanming ji*, 3.12a–b. (*Sibu congkan* ed.)

11. Sikong Tu, "Letter on Poetry to Mr. Ji Fu," in *Shipin jijie*, p. 52.

12. Su Dongpo, "Postface to the Poetry of Huang Zisi," in *Dongpo quanji*, 93.19a.

13. *Ibid.*

14. *Ibid.*

15. Wei Yingwu, "To the Daoist Master of Quanjiao Mountain," in *Wei Suzhou shiji*, 3.8a. (*Sibu beiyao* ed.)

16. "Yongye," in *Lunyu*,

17. Wang Shizhen, "Shiyou shi chuan lu," in *Qing shihua*, 2 vols., ed. Wang Fuzhi (Shanghai: Shanghai guji, 1978), vol. 1, pp. 143–44.

CHAPTER THIRTEEN: THE "MARGIN" AND THE "CENTER" OF FLAVOR

1. Su Dongpo, "Criticism of the Poetry of Han Yu and Liu Zongyuan," as

cited in Guo Shaoyu, ed., *Zhongguo lidai wenlun xuan*, 3 vols. (Hong Kong: Zhonghua shuju, 1979), vol. 2, p. 79.

2. Su Dongpo, "On Sending off the Monk Canliao," in *Dongpo quanji*, 10.11a–b.

3. Kenneth K.S. Ch'en, *Buddhism in China* (Princeton: Princeton University Press, NJ, 1964), p. 85.

4. Seng Rui, "Preface to the *Zhonglun* by Nagarjuna," in *Taishô*, 30:1a–b. For a discussion of this text, see especially Richard H. Robinson, *Early Madhyamika in India and China* (Madison: University of Wisconsin Press, 1967), p. 115.

5. Seng Zhao, "Bu zhen kong lun" in *Taishô*, 45.152a–53a. Also see Robinson, *Early Madhyamika*, p. 123; and Seng Zhao, *The Book of Chao*, trans. and ann. Walter Liebenthal, Monumenta Serica, Monograph Series 13 (Beijing: Catholic University of Beijing, 1948), p. 56.

6. Seng Zhao, "Bu zhen kong lun," 45.152a–53a.

7. See especially the commentary of this poem in the doctoral dissertation by Beata Grant, "Buddhism and Taoism in the Poetry of Su Shi" (UMI, 1987), p. 225. See also her book *Mount Lu Revisited: Buddhism in the Life and Writings of Su Shih* (Honolulu: University of Hawaii Press, 1994), pp. 97–101.

8. Su Dongpo, "On Sending off the Monk Canliao," 10.11a–b.

9. Su Dongpo, "Ciyun Canliao ji Shaoyou," in Su Shi, *Su Dongpo quanji*, 2 vols. (Taipei: He Luo tushu chubanshe, 1975), vol. 2, p. 52.

10. Su Dongpo, "Lyric: Washing Sands," in *Dongpo ci*, p. 11.

11. Proclus, *Commentaire sur la République*, trans. and ann. A.J. Festugière (Paris: J. Vrin, 1970), p. 95.

12. Silenus is the name of a deity of the woods and springs, frequent companion of Dionysus. Often represented as completely covered with hair and animal-like in appearance, he (or they, since there were many Silenuses) possessed the gift of prophecy, which he would impart only under force. — TRANS.

13. See especially the discussion in Tzvetan Todorov, *Symbolism and Interpretation*, trans. Catherine Porter (Ithaca, NY: Cornell University Press, 1982), p. 120; see also Alain Le Boulluec, "Voile et ornement: Le Texte et l'addition des

sens, selon Clément d'Alexandrie," in *Question de sens* (Paris: Presses de l'Ecole Normale Supérieure, 1982), p. 52. For a general study of the problem, see Henri de Lubac, *Medieval Exegesis*, trans. Mark Sebanc (Grand Rapids, MI: W.B. Eerdmans, 1998).

14. See "The Dharma-Door of Nonduality," in Robert A.F. Thurman, trans., *The Holy Teaching of Vimalakirti: A Mahayana Scripture* (University Park: Pennsylvania State University Press, 1976), pp. 73–77.

CHAPTER FOURTEEN: BLANDNESS OR STRENGTH

1. *Shiren yuxie*, 10.12a.

2. Su Dongpo, "Criticism of the Poetry of Han Yu and Liu Zongyuan," as cited in *Zhongguo lidai wenlun xuan*, vol. 2, p. 79. Italics mine.

3. Han Yu, "Farewell Letter to Gao Xian." For the full text, see Gao Buying, ed., *Tang Song wen juyao*, 3 vols. (Hong Kong: Zhonghua shuju, 1976), vol. 1, pp. 220–25. This important text has been studied most notably by Charles Hartman in his *Han Yü and the T'ang Search for Unity* (Princeton, NJ: Princeton University Press, 1986), pp. 222–24; and by Hsiung Ping-ming, *Zhang Xu et la calligraphie cursive folle* (Paris: Institut des Hautes Etudes Chinoises, 1984), p. 117.

4. Han Yu, "Farewell Letter to Gao Xian."

5. *Ibid.*

6. Su Dongpo, "Sending off the Monk Canliao," in *Dongpo quanji*, 10.11a–b.

7. *Ibid.*

8. Mi Fu, *Huashi*, pp. 14 and 91, in *Congshu jicheng xinbian*, vol. 53, pp. 144 and 153; also see Nicole Vandier-Nicolas, trans., *Le Houa-che de Mi Fou* (Paris: PUF, 1964), pp. 35 and 93.

9. Mi Fu, *Huashi*, p. 15; Vandier-Nicolas, *Le Houa-che de Mi Fou*, p. 36.

10. See, for example, Zhao Mengfu, "Songxue lunhua," in *Zhongguo hualun leibian*, ed. Yu Jianhua (Hong Kong: Zhonghua shuju, 1957), p. 92.

11. Li Rihua, in *Leibian*, p. 132.

12. *Ibid.*, p. 130.

13. Dai Xi, in *Leibian*, p. 992.

14. Yun Xiang, in *Leibian*, p. 769.

15. Fang Xun, in *Leibian*, p. 235.

16. *Ibid.*, p. 239.

17. *Ibid.*, p. 231.

18. *Ibid.*, p. 230.

CHAPTER FIFTEEN: TRANSCENDENCE IS NATURAL

1. André Gide, "Billet à Angèle" 1921; also see André Gide, *Incidences* (Paris, Nouvelle Revue Française, 1924), p. 40.

2. Paul Verlaine, "En Sourdine," in *Fêtes Galantes/Claude Debussy*, (Paris: J. Jobert, 1924).

3. Jean-Pierre Richard, *Poésie et profondeur* (Paris: Seuil, 1955), p. 165.

4. *Ibid.*, p. 166.

5. *Ibid.*, p. 170.

6. Vladimir Jankélévitch, *De la musique au silence: Fauré et l'inexprimable*, pp. 130 and 263.

7. Vladimir Jankélévitch, *La Musique et l'ineffable*, new ed. (Paris: Seuil, 1983), p. 65.

8. Jankélévitch, *Fauré et l'inexprimable*, p. 261.

9. Jankélévitch, *La Musique et l'ineffable*, pp. 59 and 61.

10. Jankélévitch, *Fauré et l'inexprimable*, p. 261.

11. Richard, *Poésie et profondeur*, p. 183.

12. One might think of Epinal images as "pretty pictures" or "clichéd images." More precisely, this is a reference to the well-known cheap and extremely commonplace images, lithographs, and engravings for which the town Epinal in the northeast of France is known. — TRANS.

13. Paul Verlaine, *Sagesse*, ed. C. Chadwick (London: Athlone Press, 1973), vol. 1, pp. xxii and p. 45.

Notes on Major Chinese

Figures Mentioned

Bo (or Bai) Juyi 白居 (772–846)

A poet of international renown even today, and especially popular in Japan, he was a strong proponent of the political and moral value of poetry, producing satiric verse (directed not only at society but, on occasion, even at himself) as well as poems about daily life. Composing in a straightforward, almost prosaic, style, he is often praised for having written poems that could be understood and appreciated by all, not just the elite members of the court.

Confucius 孔子 (b. ca. 552–479 B.C.E.)

Born toward the end of the violent and culturally rich period known as the "Springs and Autumns" (720–481 B.C.E.), he traveled widely, teaching his belief in human perfectibility through the cultivation of man's inborn nature. For Confucius and his followers, the ultimate goal of self-cultivation was a harmonious and just society and government; and this emphasis on man as a social being ensured that Confucian thought would ever be considered in opposition to the more spiritual ideas associated with Daoism (see Laozi and Zhuangzi). Although not appreciated by the ruling courts in his time, his teachings were disseminated by his many disciples and eventually recorded in a work known as the *Lunyu* (usually translated as the *Analects*). He can hardly be said to have developed a theory of representation, but the aphoristic quality of the language attributed to him, combined with scattered remarks on communication through language, suggests a consistent view. He believed that while words do not fully convey meaning, a discerning reader or listener will be able to detect patterns that reveal the nature and moral state of the writer or speaker. In addition, his remarks on the pedagogical value of *The Book of Odes* tell us that the words and writings produced by the members of a moral society have the power to transform their readers and hearers.

Dong Yuan 董源 / 董元 (d. 962)

Living and working during the Five Dynasties, he has been credited as one of the originators of the literati tradition of monochrome-ink landscape painting. When, during the course of the Northern Song dynasty, landscape painting grew to be the dominant genre, Dong Yuan's style was studied and imitated by the great masters of that period. Along with his most famous pupil, the Buddhist priest Juran (active ca. 960–985), he developed a wet-brush technique that, applied to monumental scenes, earned them recognition as the two great masters of Jiangnan (southern) landscape. Typical of what came to be known as the Southern school, Dong Yuan's and Juran's paintings strove to imbue their landscapes with emotion, in contrast with the Northern school's preference for colorful, monumental, and objective renderings of specific landscapes.

Du Fu 董源 / 董元 (712–770)

Often referred to as one of China's two greatest poets (along with Li Bo), he was most admired for his subtle mastery of virtually every poetic form, his deep knowledge of the literary tradition, and his intense, almost wrenching empathy for the sufferings of the people. His poems are much admired for the subtle and complex interplay between linguistic structures and poetic forms (especially parallelism); yet his sophisticated handling of language only enhances the impression they convey of authenticity and unmediated expression.

Han Yu 韓愈 (768–824)

One of the earliest proponents, and certainly the best known, of the so-called "ancient prose" movement, which favored returning to an "ancient" style that emphasized content (especially Confucian content) over form, this accomplished essayist and poet composed many didactic, almost vernacular poems in the spirit of his convictions. Later in life, during a period of political difficulties, he blended straightforward language with an unaccustomed use of supernatural images and strikingly original phrasing, resulting in evocative if somewhat hermetic work.

Juran 巨然 *See* Dong Yuan.

Laozi 老子 (n.d.)

Precious little is known about the historical Laozi, a figure who, if he did exist, is thought to have been a contemporary of Confucius's. Most important, his name is synonymous with the patriarch of Daoism and is closely associated with the foundational Daoist text known as both the *Laozi* and the *Dao de jing* (the earliest extant fragments of which can be reliably dated at around 300 B.C.). This text of eighty-one "chapters" largely comprises pithy, aphoristic statements that attempt to convey an understanding of the ineffable, indefinable Dao, or "Way," the underlying principle of change and transformation that governs the natural world and human existence. The sage — and especially the sage-ruler — is taught to live life in perfect harmony with the Dao, adopting an attitude of lucid "non-action" and thereby setting an example that will naturally be followed by others.

Li Bo (or Bai) 李白 (701–762) Often referred to as the "Banished Immortal," he has endured, alongside Du Fu (if at times rather precariously), in the upper strata of the poetic pantheon. A controversial and colorful personality, he produced a body of work most often characterized as "unfettered," "inimitable," and, in short, anything but bland. Detractors have begrudgingly acknowledged his prodigious talent but — using his unabashed admirer Du Fu as foil — complain of his disregard (or even ignorance) of poetic tradition, his seemingly gratuitous reliance on Daoist mystical imagery for effect, and his self-absorbed inattention to the plight of the people.

Liu Gongquan 柳公權 (778–865)

A highly ranked official and scholar of Confucian classics, he established a calligraphic style that became the most prestigious of his times: firm, four-square individualized characters composed of sharp angles and clearly defined, weighty strokes. He made the telling claim that his style consisted of the combined elements of a long list of earlier calligraphy masters, including Zhong You and Wang Xizhi.

Liu Zongyuan 柳宗原 (773–819)

Renowned as a great essayist, he worked in the "ancient prose" style; appreciated for his nature poetry, he was influenced by such poets as Wang Wei and Wei Yingwu. His best-known work was written during his years in exile in the remote southern region of Liuzhou (modern-day Guangxi Province), exhibiting the influence of Daoist and Buddhist thought, even as he never ceased seeing himself as a loyal Confucian.

Lu Ji 陸機 (261–303)

A prolific poet, he is today best known for his authorship of "Wen fu" (Poetic exposition on literature), the earliest extant work to explore the process of poetic creativity at length. Among the issues he so memorably raises in this piece are inspiration, originality, and the relationship between language and the world.

Mei Yaochen 梅堯臣 (1002–1060; also known as Mei Shengshu 梅聖)

A close friend of Ouyang Xiu's, he is best known for his introduction of the "plain and bland" aesthetic into lyric poetry, embracing both simplicity in language and attention to the details of everyday experience.

Mencius 孟子 (ca. 371–ca. 289 B.C.E.)

Teaching doctrines derived from those of Confucius, he developed them further in his belief that man's nature is originally and innately good and that one must strive to retrieve and cultivate that originally good heart and mind. He stood in strong opposition to both the Mohist doctrine of universal love and the Legalist doctrine that man is innately evil. His eponymous work was included by the Song dynasty philosopher Zhu Xi in the *Four Books*.

Mi Fu (or Fei) 米芾 (1052–1107)

An eccentric painter, calligrapher, collector, and connoisseur, he typified the seamless blending of high erudition and spontaneous, unpredictable creativity, producing script that has been described as close to modern abstract painting.

Ni Zan 倪瓚 (1301?–1374)

A literati painter whose early life of privilege was radically transformed by a combination of natural disaster and political upheaval in the years leading up to the fall of the Yuan dynasty, he is most often associated with the painting of landscapes in a spare, unadorned, lofty style, which he developed in the latter part of his career. The vicissitudes of his life have contributed to the widespread interpretation of his work as expressive of his inner loftiness of spirit.

Ouyang Xiu 歐陽修 (1007–1072)

A renowned prose stylist, poet, historian, and statesman of firm Confucian principles, he produced writings that range widely in both style and genre. A not unconditional admirer of Han Yu, he favored and promoted a natural and unadorned approach to writing and scholarship, assuming a stance that placed him in opposition to current political trends and resulted in his periodic exile to remote posts.

Ruan Ji 阮籍 (210–263)

An official of the failing Wei dynasty and close friend of the ruling family, he expressed in his haunting, intensely personal, and often abstruse poetry his sorrow at the usurpation of the throne and his frustration at living in unstable and unsavory political times. Ultimately seeking knowledge and understanding in Daoist mysticism, he is remembered (along with his cohorts who make up the "Seven Sages of the Bamboo Grove") as a wild Daoist eccentric and, as one scholar refers to him, "a poet's poet."

Sikong Tu 司空圖 (837–908)

A rarely anthologized but well-known poet of the late Tang dynasty, he is best known for his work *Ershi si shipin* (Twenty-four poetic modes). This influential cycle of poems, unique in the tradition of Chinese poetic criticism, is devoted to setting down, in suggestive, evocative terms, the complete range of lyric modes encompassed in poetic expression.

Su Dongpo 蘇東破 (1037–1101; also called Su Shi 蘇軾)

A brilliantly inventive master of virtually all literary forms, he was also a courageous political critic who spent much of his life exiled to provincial posts (indeed, the name "Dongpo," or "Eastern Slope," was originally that of his farm in Huangzhou). Traditional critics often describe his poetry as "boundless" and "unfettered," adjectives typically applied to his much-admired Tang predecessor Li Bo.

Tao Yuanming 陶淵明 (365–427; also called Tao Qian 陶潛)

Perhaps the earliest poet to be associated, if only in retrospect, with the aesthetic of the "plain and bland," he wrote poems that express, in the simplest of language and images, the precarious joys and physical hardships of one who made the difficult decision to reject life as an official and live in retirement in the "fields and farms." While some of his poems are overtly philosophical, his poetic legacy (first established by Du Fu over three centuries after his death) derives from those that integrate his Daoism in verse about (mostly subsistence) farming, the pleasures of wine, and the fruits and trials that come of heeding one's own nature.

Wang Meng 王蒙 (ca. 1308–1385; also known as the Firewood Gatherer of the Yellow Crane Mountain)

A painter whose name is often mentioned in contrast with Ni Zan, he lived a life rocked by political upheaval, ultimately dying in prison after having been implicated in a treasonous scandal. His landscape painting is strongly reminiscent of the earlier monumental, ordered style of the Northern school (see entry on

Dong Yuan), but he imbues those scenes with surprising, energizing arrangements of light and shadow and unnatural distortions of shapes and proportions.

Wang Wei 王維 (ca. 701–761)

Retroactively dubbed the patriarch of the Southern school style of painting exemplified by Dong Yuan and Juran, this poet and painter imbued his works with a Chan Buddhist–inspired sensitivity to the "emptiness" of all things. While his paintings had disappeared by the time of the Northern Song dynasty, his landscape poetry — most notably that inspired by his estate at Wangchuan — earned him the status of one of the great Tang poets. Particularly striking is his ability to convey the subjective relativity of perception and the ultimate unity of all things.

Wang Xizhi 王羲之 (307–ca. 365)

Born into an illustrious family of Shandong that was forced to flee to the south during the nomad invasions that occurred subsequent to the fall of the Han dynasty, he immersed himself in neo-Daoist and Buddhist thought and in the practice of poetry and calligraphy. He is credited with having revolutionized Chinese calligraphy, single-handedly transforming it from the ritualized expression of political legitimacy into a potent mode of self-expression. His running script in particular stands in eloquent contrast to the previously dominant monumental clerical style, more accurately characterized as traces of the subtle, expressive movements of a hand that is ever in tune with his inner being.

Wei Yingwu 韋應物 (737–ca. 792)

Although not especially popular in his time, he gradually came to be recognized as one of the literary descendants of Tao Yuanming, composing poems inspired by natural scenes in language that is unadorned and contemplative. Adept at writing regulated verse, he is most appreciated for his mastery of the pentasyllabic ancient style and was greatly admired by the avatar of the "plain and bland" in poetry, Mei Yaochen.

Yan Zhenqing 顏真卿 (709–785)

A high-ranking official who staunchly defended the Tang court against rebel insurgents until he died at their hands, he wrote a monumental, solid calligraphy in large standard script that marks a turning away from the more sophisticated, Wang Xizhi–inspired calligraphy that had been favored by the Tang court. His rounded brushwork and strong lines convey a steady, forward-moving energy, balanced by his unique ability to integrate the various components of complex characters into one harmonious pattern. Su Dongpo would later cite him as having brought calligraphy to its apogee, exhausting the possibilities inherent in the technical variations of earlier forms.

Zhang Xu 張旭 (fl. ca. 700–750)

Along with the wandering monk Huaisu (ca. 735–ca. 799), he is recognized as an originator of the wild-cursive script and enjoyed performing his art before elite audiences. Contemporary poets Li Bo and Du Fu praised him as a calligrapher whose characters seemed the very embodiment of dynamism and spontaneity.

Zhong Hong (or Rong) 鍾嶸 (ca. 465–518)

Although not a poet, he left an indelible mark on the history of Chinese poetry in the form of a work known as the *Shipin* 詩品 , the earliest attempt to systematically evaluate individual lyric poets according to clearly articulated standards within the context of literary history. Each of the 122 poets he reviews is assigned one of three ranks, with the highest rank reserved for poets who effectively express, in striking language, genuine feelings stirred by experiences in the world. He describes this standard in his preface, where he asserts the need for balance between figurative and descriptive language.

Zhong You 鍾繇 (151–230)

The first master of early standard script, he worked during the period when calligraphy began to be appreciated for its own aesthetic qualities. He is the earliest calligrapher whose style can be reliably reconstructed today.

Zhuangzi 莊子 (third century B.C.E; Zhuang Zhou 莊周)

Long associated with Laozi as a virtual co-founder of what we now think of as Daoist thought, he devised colorful, imaginative parables that emphasize the necessity of cleaving to one's inner nature, comprehending the relativity of perception and understanding, and adapting to the world as one finds it. The eponymous work *Zhuangzi* contains thirty-three chapters, but only the first seven "inner chapters" are accepted as possibly being from his own hand.

Zhu Xi 朱熹 (1130–1200)

Perhaps the greatest and most influential Chinese thinker since the Warring States philosophers Confucius, Mencius, Laozi, and Zhuangzi, he synthesized central Confucian ideas with those originating in *yin-yang* and five-elements theory, reenergizing Confucianism by infusing it with a spiritual dimension. His annotated edition of the *Four Books* (*Analects, Mencius, Doctrine of the Middle Way, Great Learning*) became the basis of the civil-service examinations from the fourteenth through the beginning of the twentieth century.

APPENDIX B

Glossary of Chinese Expressions

benmo 本末
bian 邊
buji buli 不即不離
caixing 才性
cheng 成
chengdan jingzhi 澄澹精緻
chongdan 沖淡
chu guan pingdan, jiu shi shen ming 初觀平淡，久視神明
congming 聰明
dan 淡
danbo xianyuan 淡泊閒遠
dannong 淡濃
dansu 淡俗
de 德
dianya 典雅
gan dong 感動
gan tong 感通
gao feng jue chen 高風絕塵
jing 境
jing 精
jingshen 精神

jueju 絕句

junzi zhi dao dan er bu yan 君子之道淡而不厭

ke 客

kui 虧

mo 漠

pian 偏

pin 品

pingdan suimei 平淡邃美

pingdan tianran 平淡天然

pingdan tianzhen 平淡天真

pingdan wuwei 平淡無味

qi 齐

qili 綺麗

qing 清

qingli xiansi pingdan 清麗閒肆平淡

qingqi 清奇

qingxu 清虛

ren 仁

shen 神

shen wei zhi 深味之

tian 天

tiwei 體味

tong 通

wei / wuwei 為 / 無為

xian er shang 絃而上

xiang 象

xiannong 纖穠

xiangwai zhi xiang, jingwai zhi jing 象外之象，景外之景

xin 信

xing 興

xionghun 雄渾

yan 艷

yin 音
yiyin/yiwei 遺音 / 遺味
zhen 真
zheng 徵
zheng 正
zhong 中

Designed by Bruce Mau with Sarah Dorkenwald
Typeset by Archetype
Printed and bound by Maple-Vail